THE MASTER TELLS STORIES
VOLUME 2

THE MASTER TELLS STORIES

VOLUME 2

BY DHARMA MASTER CHENG YEN

Translated by Norman Yuan, Lin Sen-Shou,
Wu Hsiao-ting and Liao Yi-chen
English edited by Douglas Shaw and Hu
Tsung-hsiang

Tzu Chi Cultural Publishing Company

The Master Tells Stories
Volume Two

Published by the Tzu Chi Cultural Publishing Co.
No. 19, Alley 7, Lane 217,
Chunghsiao E. Road, Sec. 3, Taipei, Taiwan, Rep. of China
Telephone: 886-2-2887-0111
Fax: 886-2-2776-0514
E-mail: kp_liu@tzuchi.org.tw

First edition, March 2001
Second printing March 2002
Printed in Taiwan, Republic of China

Publisher: Shih Cheng Yen
Director of Tzu Chi Cultural Mission: Wang Tuan-cheng
Editor-in-chief: Liu King-pong
Translation by Norman Yuan, Lin Sen-shou, Wu Hsiao-
ting and Liao Yi-chen
English editing by Douglas Shaw and Hu Tsung-hsiang
Cover design by Chang Shih-ming
Inside art by Chang Su-hua

ISBN: 957-8300-75-1

CONTENTS

SECTION 4: THE ANIMALS SHOW GRATITUDE

SECTION 5: THE YOUNG MAN AND THE FIVE TURTLES

SECTION 6: THE LOVE OF ALL LIVING BEINGS

Section 1
The Busy Brother

The Busy Brother

Life is impermanent. The most reliable way of living is to use this very moment to do whatever is right.

There is a story in one of the Buddhist sutras. There were two brothers who grew up together, each with his own ideals. After their parents passed away, the younger one, searching for the meaning of life, left home to conduct his spiritual cultivation. He let his brother take complete charge of the business left by their parents.

After several years of ascetic living, the younger brother realized that life was impermanent, that all fame and wealth were illusory, and that good deeds must be performed without delay. He wished that his brother could experience the same enlightenment.

He went home and told his brother what he had come to understand over the past years. But his brother was very serious about managing the business and was busy all the time. "You have done well in your spiritual cultivation, and what you have said is very reasonable. But I have a heavy responsibility which I cannot ignore."

"You control your own time, so you should spare a little time to seek the truth of life," said the younger brother.

"My business is very big and there are many things that I have to attend to myself," responded the older brother. "How can I spare any time?"

"If you have no time, you can spare some money to help the poor and needy."

"When I have more money, I'll do that."

No matter how his brother advised him, the businessman always gave him all kinds of excuses.

Seeing that his brother could not be convinced, the younger one was very disappointed and left home to continue his spiritual cultivation.

Several years later, the practitioner heard that his brother had died. Deeply grieved, he went into deep meditation to try and find out where his brother was. He searched through Heaven and the Human World, but there was no sign of him. He entered Hell and the Realm of Hungry Ghosts, but there was no trace of him there, either. Finally he entered the Animal Realm. There he found his brother, who had become a buffalo.

He woke up from his meditation and hurried back to his hometown. There he found his brother, the buffalo, painfully dragging a plough through a muddy field. The fatigued animal was plodding along more and more slowly, which prompted its master to keep whipping it. The buffalo wore a sad expression as if to tell people it could not last much longer.

The younger brother saw that the buffalo was at the point of complete exhaustion, yet its master never relented. The practitioner couldn't help sighing. "You were busy all your life when you were a human being," he said to the buffalo. "You had no time to do any good deeds, so you accumulated a lot of bad karma which you carried with you to this animal life. I hope you can reflect on your life now and free yourself from this cycle of reincarnation."

It seemed as if the buffalo understood what the practitioner had said. Suddenly it struggled and started wailing. Then it fell to the ground and died. Seeing the strange incident, other farmers gathered around the master of the buffalo and asked him what had happened.

"I also think it is very strange," the master said. "Just a few minutes ago, a Buddhist practitioner stood here murmuring to himself and my buffalo suddenly started wailing. It struggled for a while, and then it fell to the ground and died."

All the farmers suspected that the practitioner might have played some magic trick. Otherwise, how could the buffalo have died? They surrounded the young man and demanded an explanation. "The buffalo was my brother in his previous life," he told them. "I always advised him to do good deeds, but he invariably gave me excuses, saying he was too busy. However, life is impermanent, and he died before he found time to do good deeds. After he died, he fell into the Animal Realm and became a buffalo. As a buffalo, he was still busy, painfully pulling a plough. In life, when does one really have any leisure time? You should make the best use of your time, take every opportunity to do good deeds and find time to quiet down for spiritual cultivation." Through his words, the farmers achieved a certain understanding.

In summary, life is impermanent. You should seize this very moment to do what ought to be done. If you have the wrong priorities, your life will be ridden with craving and anxieties. Then you will never be able to attain emancipation from the suffering and the cycle of reincarnation.

Efficacious
or Inefficacious

Greed is the cause of poverty. If we have no desire in our hearts, we can avoid the distress caused by unsatisfied cravings.

here was once a village in Japan. To the east was a tall mountain and to the west, a broad plain. One day an old man came to this village. He was carrying two statues of the Earth Treasury Bodhisattva, one before him and the other on his back. "Do you know how old I am?" he called out. "I am 330 years old, and I have been carrying these two statues for over two hundred years…"

The villagers gathered around him, and he continued. "I am going to find places to settle these two statues so that people can worship them. One of them is most efficacious. Whatever you ask of him, you will get. The other one is totally unresponsive and will not answer any of your prayers. I am going to place the inefficacious one on the plain and pave a road so that people will find it easy to reach him. As to the efficacious one, I will put him in the high mountains. Because he gives whatever anyone asks, people will find a way to reach him no matter how difficult or dangerous it is."

The old man placed the statues as he had said. Very few people went to worship the inefficacious bodhisattva even though the road was wide and easy to travel on. On the other hand, droves of people continuously made their way up the high mountain to worship the efficacious bodhisattva. The original mountain path, which had been full of grass, twigs and rattan, became a wide road because it was so frequently treaded on. That statue was truly efficacious. Whoever asked for good health got good health; whoever wished for wealth got wealth. Therefore, many incense sticks and candles burned there.

Three decades later, all the villagers were rich and enjoyed good health. Then some people thought, "This kind of life is too dull—I must find a way to be richer than the others." So they began to beg the bodhisattva to make the other villagers poor and sick. As the bodhisattva was always efficacious, such curses came true too.

After another twenty years, the villagers were even worse off than they had been fifty years before. They had become lazy because whatever they wanted they were granted by simply praying to the efficacious bodhisattva. They never had to work anymore and so had all but lost their ability to make a living. So when poverty struck again, they had nothing to fall back on. Their helplessness was aggravated by their mutual cursing, and the villagers lived in miserable destitution.

One hundred years later, the same old man appeared in the village again. "The efficacious bodhisattva is not necessarily good for people," he told the villagers. "People are insatiably greedy and often do things that are harmful to others and no good for themselves. Such greed is the cause of poverty. Now you should worship the inefficacious bodhisattva with a sincere heart. He may not give you what you want, but he won't harm you either. What you need is to build up your faith without asking for anything in return."

Because it never responded to prayers, the other statue of the Earth Treasury Bodhisattva had not been worshipped for over a century. The road that led to the statue was covered with grass and it took the old man a long time to find the statue. Now the people no longer went up the mountain to worship the efficacious bodhisattva. Instead, they sincerely went to worship the inefficacious one. Since they had no inordinate cravings anymore, they worked hard and gradually improved their lives.

After a few years, the village once more became quite prosperous. The villagers worked hard and respected each other, and they lived peacefully and at ease.

Some people are always asking for more. Even when they are rich, they want to be even richer so they can outshine others. In order to reach their objective, they don't care if they have to harm others. That is the mindset of common people in this world.

It is much better to help yourself than to ask for help from the bodhisattvas. Do the best you can and you will accomplish a great deal. In addition, you should maintain a mind that wants nothing. When you do not want anything, you will not agonize over unfulfilled desires. Happiness will arrive only when one is content!

Killing the Tiger

In our daily conduct, we must humble ourselves and be courteous to others. In this way, we will avoid hindrances.

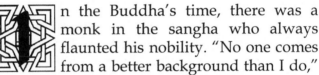n the Buddha's time, there was a monk in the sangha who always flaunted his nobility. "No one comes from a better background than I do," he said. "My family is the richest in the country. Before I became a monk, I ate the best food, wore the best clothes and used the best things. Even the things my servant used were imported..." Every time this monk came back from begging for alms, he looked at the coarse food in his bowl and said with a sigh, "What fine food I had in the past! Look at the food I have now." Hearing such complaints day after day, the other monks began to grumble about him.

When the Buddha heard about this, he told the sangha the story of this monk.

This monk had the same habit of being arrogant a long, long time ago in a previous life. He used to be a weaver, tall and handsome. At that time, there was a very clever craftsman who not only made very good bows and arrows but was also a first class marksman. In every marksmanship contest, he was the champion.

Versatile as he was, he wanted to contribute to his country. Unfortunately he was very short and not very impressive as far as appearances went, and he was afraid the king would look down on him.

Therefore he wanted to find a tall, handsome young man to visit the king with him. Finally, he found the weaver. "Let's go to see the king together," he said. "You tell him that you're a good marksman and I'm your servant. If the king employs us, then we'll never have to worry again."

The weaver thought it was indeed a very good opportunity, so he agreed. They went to the palace to see the king, who was pleased to see them and offered them a generous stipend. Thereafter they lived a very comfortable life.

Not long after, the news began to circulate that a tiger had been seen near the main road leading to the city gate and that it had already killed several people. The king summoned the weaver and told him to get rid of the tiger. Assigned such a dangerous mission, the weaver was worried that his true identity might be disclosed. He discussed with his servant what to do.

"Don't be frightened," the craftsman said to the weaver. "You must keep calm. First of all, you have to announce the exact time that you are going to go hunt the tiger. When the time comes, people will come with bows and arrows to help. Then you must go to the haunt of the tiger and let it follow you to where all the people are gathered. When it does, hide behind a bush. Out of fear, all the people will shoot the tiger with their bows and arrows. When the tiger has been shot, stand up with a rope in your hand and tell everyone that you had intended to catch the tiger alive. Demand that the person who rashly killed the tiger come forward. I am sure no one will dare to admit it. Then you can carry the dead tiger to the king, who will certainly be very happy and bestow upon you a handsome award."

The weaver did exactly what his servant told him to do. Sure enough, the tiger was shot to death and the king gave the weaver a great deal of treasure.

After some time, a wild ox appeared and also threatened the people. Using the same method as for the tiger, the weaver got rid of the wild ox. Again the king gave him many rewards and trusted him all the more.

Having eliminated both the tiger and the wild ox and won the trust of the king, the weaver became arrogant and no longer respected the craftsman. "Don't forget, you are my servant. You are supposed to serve me." The craftsman could only wait patiently.

Another period of time passed until one day the neighboring countries suddenly ganged up to attack this country. The first person to come to the king's mind was the weaver. "Since you are such an outstanding marksman, I order you to fight the first battle." The weaver was half-pleased and half-worried, because if he won the battle he would be promoted to a higher position and gain both fame and wealth, but if he lost he would lose everything.

The closer the enemy forces drew, the more fearful the weaver became. Worried about what he might do, his servant followed him closely.

On his departure, the weaver sat on the back of an elephant, looking very impressive. But when the enemy arrived, he was so scared that he wet his pants and almost fell off the elephant's back. His servant tied him to the elephant with a rope and said, "When you were in power, you were so flushed with pride! Now in the face of the enemy you are so frightened. How pathetic! Go back and clean yourself up and leave the enemy to me."

So the weaver went back, leaving his short servant to fight the battle. With his excellent marksmanship and tactical skill, the craftsman quickly led the army to victory.

Returning from the battlefield, the craftsman went to the king under his true identity. The king was very happy, but he also regretted that such an outstanding man had been neglected for such a long time just because he felt inferior for being short. The king put him in command of his army. After the battle, the weaver lost all his arrogance.

The Buddha continued, "And guess what? This monk used to be that weaver. He was born into a low caste and feels inferior. Being arrogant is his way of concealing his inferiority complex."

Whether in studying Buddhism or getting along with other people, you must humble yourselves and treat others with respect. Always be modest. If you are filled with arrogance and pride, you will encounter many obstacles on the road of spiritual cultivation and in life.

Prince Virudhaka

Hatred is a horrible mindset. When anger fills the heart, 84,000 anxieties follow.

ore than two thousand years ago (about ten years after the Buddha was enlightened), India was divided into several small states. The Buddha returned to Kapilavastu, where he had been born, to preach. Because of his supreme achievement, everyone in India thought the Sakyas were a caste of ultimate wisdom. [The Buddha was also called Sakyamuni, "the sage of the Sakyas."] They believed anyone who married one of the Sakyas would have offspring that were endowed with strong intellectual powers. In a small country called Kosala, Prensenajit had just succeeded to the throne. He thought of taking a Sakya woman as his bride, so he sent a minister to the Sakyas to convey his intention.

When the minister arrived at Kapilavastu, it so happened that five hundred ministers of the country were having a meeting, so he told the five hundred ministers the young king's wish. The ministers discussed the issue. Some of them had no respect for that king. They thought they were the best caste, and so none of them want-

ed to give him their daughters in marriage.
Some even hurled abuse at him: "Who does he
think he is? How dare he think of taking one of
our girls as his wife?"

One of the ministers, named Mahanan,
calmly expressed his opinion to the others.
"Prensenajit is young and proud. He is also
very hot-tempered. We'd better be careful not
to offend him. We must find a way to appease
both sides. You can leave the problem to me."
On his way back home, he noticed that one of
his servants had a very beautiful daughter
named Mallika. An idea suddenly occurred to
him — he adopted that girl and married her to
Prensenajit in a grand wedding.

Because of her beauty, the young king
loved her very much. Lady Mallika was very
graceful and prudent. One year later, she
delivered a lovely son. Prensenajit was very
pleased and asked a Brahman teacher to
name the boy. The teacher named him Prince
Virudhaka.

The prince was very clever and everybody
loved him dearly. When he was eight or nine
years old, his father wanted to send him to
Kapilavastu to learn different skills from the
Sakyas. He said to the boy, "You have to learn
the six arts so that you can be a good king
when you grow up. I'll send you back to your
mother's country where intellectualism thrives

and the six arts [rites, music, archery, chariot driving, reading and mathematics] are highly developed." Prince Virudhaka was very glad to do as his father told him, and he departed with his retinue.

When Mahanan learned the purpose of Prince Virudhaka's trip, he arranged for a group of young boys to accompany him and study the arts with him. At that time, Kapilavastu was building a magnificent lecture hall for the Buddha, and they had prepared a splendid chair in the center of the lecture hall. When Prince Virudhaka and his retinue happened to pass by, he saw the magnificent lecture hall and he went inside to look around.

Out of curiosity, he sat on that splendid-looking chair. Just then, the minister supervising the construction came inside and saw the young prince sitting on the chair. Angered, he dragged the boy off the chair and reproached him: "You son of a maid! How dare you defile the Buddha's seat!" He shoved the prince out of the lecture hall, scolding him relentlessly with nasty words.

That incident planted a hatred in Prince Virudhaka's heart that was never to be removed. He told his aide, "You must remember the insults I suffered today and remind me always so that I can avenge myself one day. If I forget, you can remind me three times a day."

Prince Virudhaka returned to his own country with that hatred planted deep in his heart. When he became king, he ordered his army to destroy the Sakyas.

Hatred is a horrible mindset. It is the cause of much ruin. We must carefully cultivate our minds in daily life. We mustn't defame others, even unintentionally, nor should we bury hatred in our hearts. If we do, the seed of hatred will emerge once our minds go astray and the consequences will be irredeemable. If we have an accommodating mind and cultivate ourselves at all times, then we will not have evil thoughts or do harm to others.

Ananda's Regret

It would be better to live only one day and understand the dharma than to live a hundred years without knowing it.

nanda, a cousin of the Buddha, was one of his top ten disciples. As the Buddha's attendant, Ananda was always by his side. Because of his excellent memory, Ananda was famed for hearing and remembering the Buddha's teachings, and so he was known as his most learned disciple.

After the Buddha attained nirvana, the sangha held a meeting to compile his teachings. Ananda was elected as the representative to recite and pass on the teachings orally.

Time passed and Ananda became old. At that time, religious practitioners learned the Buddhist teachings by word of mouth. One day, Ananda came to the Abode of the Bamboo Grove. He heard a young monk reciting one of the Buddha's verses as, "It would be better to live only one day and see a crane than to live a hundred years without seeing one."

Hearing this, Ananda's heart sank. He felt sad and anxious, wondering why the correct dharma through which people could see the Truth had disappeared so quickly and why the

Buddha's teachings, compiled at the assembly and propagated by word of mouth, had become so full of error, bias and delusion. If the dharma continued to be passed on in this manner, it would be like someone who had gone astray leading others in the same wrong direction. How awful that would be!

Thinking about the serious consequences of misleading people, Ananda felt the responsibility to set things straight. So he went to the young monk and asked him to recite that verse once again. "That is wrong," Ananda said after the recitation. "The correct reading is, 'It would be better to live only one day and understand the dharma than to live a hundred years without knowing it.' That is the correct way, the way the Buddha taught us."

The young monk was willing to accept the correction and changed his recitation accordingly. One day his teacher heard him and asked, "What happened? You now recite the verse in a different way. Who told you to change it?"

"It was Reverend Ananda who told me the correct version," replied the young monk.

"Ananda is old and his memory is fading," his teacher said. "You'd better recite the verse the way I taught you." So the young monk went back to chanting the verse the old way again.

Ananda learned that the young monk had reverted to reciting the wrong version of the verse and asked him why he had done so. "My teacher says you are old and your memory is fading," the young monk said. "Perhaps you remembered it incorrectly. He told me to chant it the way he taught me."

Ananda was greatly saddened and discouraged. He thought of how the correct teachings had been spoken through the Buddha's mouth, repeated by himself, and compiled in the assembly. Now, while he was still alive, the verse was already being chanted the wrong way. If even his words could not be trusted, he couldn't imagine what was going to happen in the future. Faced with such a problem, Ananda felt entirely hopeless and contemplated leaving the world.

The inaccurate chanting of the verse could not be corrected even while Ananda was still alive, not to mention what would happen after his death. Furthermore, since the Buddhist teachings have been passed down for more than two thousand years, it would be truly difficult for them to be entirely accurate.

Now when we study Buddhism, we have to use our wisdom to spread the Buddha's spirit in the world. We have to remember: "Great compassion is what we want to live with; the garment of gentleness and endurance is what we want to wear; we should have a thorough understanding of the Way of life, yet without clinging to it; that is all we should observe." If we can conduct our spiritual cultivation based on these principles, we will not veer too far off from the essential spirit of the principles the Buddha wanted to convey to us.

The Practitioner and the Ghost

When does the vicious circle of reprisal come to an end? Every action has its karma. Good or evil will manifest itself when the opportunity comes.

There is a story in a Buddhist sutra. Thirty kilometers from the city of Sravasti in India, there lived a Buddhist practitioner. Every day he went to beg for alms in the city, where a butcher was very kind and generous to him. Each time the butcher would give him a lot of food and daily necessities.

After his death, the butcher fell to the lower realms of reincarnation and became an underwater ghost in the Ganges River. He was frequently cut and wounded by knives and axes that fell into the river, and he was in constant pain.

He thought that this treatment was unfair because he always gave generously when he was alive. Why should he fall into the Ghost Realm after his death? He guessed that it might be from his karma for having killed too much.

"Whenever the practitioner asked me for something, I always obliged," he thought. "He knew I was a butcher. Why didn't he tell me that slaughtering animals created bad karma?" The butcher didn't blame himself for his wrongdoing. Instead he put the blame on the practitioner, and he waited in the river for an opportunity to get revenge.

Finally, his chance came. The practitioner was crossing the river on a boat. When the boat was in the middle of the river, the butcher's ghost appeared. He tugged violently at the boat, trying to turn it over. A sage also happened to be on that boat. Seeing the angry ghost, he asked, "Why are you dragging the boat down?"

The angry ghost pointed at the practitioner. "It is all because of him," he said with rage. "I gave him all the alms he wanted when I was alive. He knew very well that killing was wrong, but he never admonished me. So I fell into the Ghost Realm and now I endure excruciating pain every day. I am going to drag this practitioner into the water and let him experience what I have been going through. Or else I will just turn the whole boat over."

"Think it over carefully," the sage replied calmly. "The suffering you feel now is due to the karma from the killing you did when you were alive. If you are still harboring that kind of enmity and want to hurt the practitioner, you will build up much more bad karma and endure much more suffering. Since you know that bad karma results in ruin, why don't you change your ways now? Release your enmity, let go of your hatred. You shall be emancipated right away. As to the practitioner who did not remind you that killing brings retribution, he has created his own bad karma and will have to take the consequences."

"He is right," the ghost thought. "I should forget my vengeance and let go of my hatred. Everything has its karma. I should accept the consequences for what I have done in the past and no longer do harm to anyone." With this mindset, he had repentance in his heart and all his hatred disappeared. He held his palms together toward the sage in a gesture of reverence. Suddenly he was freed from the Ghost Realm and flew lightly away. He had been emancipated.

"Good begets good, evil begets evil." That is the law of cause and effect which all of us must understand. We have to mind our speech and behavior and do good deeds every day. When we see others doing bad deeds, we must admonish them tactfully — that is also our duty. Whenever we do something wrong, we must make corrections immediately. We must never blame others for what we have done. By living this way, we will improve our own fates.

The Stick of a Fool

At the end of our lives, are we going to take with us the evil karma of greed, anger and delusion, or are we going to take the good karma of transcendent pureness?

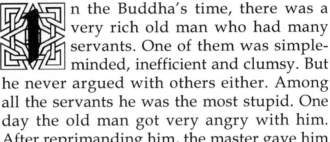n the Buddha's time, there was a very rich old man who had many servants. One of them was simple-minded, inefficient and clumsy. But he never argued with others either. Among all the servants he was the most stupid. One day the old man got very angry with him. After reprimanding him, the master gave him a stick and said, "I give you this stick because of your stupidity. If someday you meet someone who is more stupid than you, give him this stick."

Saddened, the servant took the stick. He thought, "Am I really as stupid as my master says? Is there anyone more stupid than me to whom I can give this stick?"

From then on, he took the stick every day and asked himself, "Why am I so stupid?" However, because of his simple-mindedness, he still led his life as he always had.

One day the master suddenly became very ill and had to stay in bed. All the servants stood around waiting for him to utter his last words, the stupid servant among them. Seeing all his family members and servants there, the master said, "Now I must leave you — I am going away."

"Master, where are you going?" asked the stupid servant.

"I may go to a place far, far away from here," said the master.

"Where is that place?"

"Possibly another world."

"Have you prepared your things?"

"No, I'm not going to take anything with me," replied the old man with a trace of uncertainty in his voice.

The servant took out the stick and gave it to him. "Master, you're going to such a faraway place, yet you haven't prepared anything. Isn't that very dangerous? I think you are stupid too. I give you this stick. It will help you on your journey."

Ordinarily, we only notice the stupidity of others. We always think we are smarter than others in dealing with people and events. Actually, we may be the stupid ones, only we are not aware of it. When we die, do we really not take anything with us? In fact, we do. What we take is our own karma.

Have we ever thought carefully whether we are going to take with us the evil karma of greed, anger and delusion or the good karma of transcendent pureness into the next life?

Section 2
The Buddha and the Beggar

The Buddha
and the Beggar

Compassionate love and care are essential to being a decent human being.

ne day during his stay at the Jetavana Park [a lecture hall and residence constructed for the Buddha and the sangha] in Kosala, the Buddha led his disciples out to beg for alms. In the city, they saw a group of people gathered in an alley. The Buddha sent a disciple to find out what was going on.

The disciple returned and said, "Reverend Buddha, those people are standing around an old man and talking among themselves."

"What are they talking about?" asked the Buddha.

"The old man is begging for food. He is attracting attention because he is very dirty and smells terrible. Some people even cover their noses while standing by him and pointing at him."

The Buddha walked over to the old man and asked him kindly, "How old are you, sir?"

"I am seventy years old," the old man wheezed.

"Were you born so poor?"

"No, I had a happy time growing up and was successful in my middle age. But now I am old and sick. I cannot work anymore and there is no one who can look after me. This is why I have ended up begging for a living."

"My family was very rich when I was a child," the old man continued. "When I grew up, I didn't understand that I should treasure what I had and so I lived extravagantly. This is why I am so poor today."

"What did you like doing most and how did you lead your life when you were young?" asked the Buddha.

"I liked singing and dancing and I indulged myself heavily in such pleasures."

"Can you sing and dance now?"

"I have difficulty just talking. How can I sing? I have a hunched back and clumsy hands and feet. How could I possibly dance?"

"What are the other reasons that have made you so poor?"

"One year a big flood ruined my land. The fields that had been so fertile could no longer produce any crops because they were covered with silt and gravel after the waters receded. The following year my house burned down. My wife and children died and left me alone for the rest of my life. There are many things that I regret: I regret that I did not work hard when I was young, and I regret that I indulged in drinking and womanizing in my middle age. Now I have to accept the consequences."

After hearing the old man's life story, the Buddha looked around at the people who were either covering their noses or pointing at the old beggar. "Men are not born old, and rich men are not always rich," he said to them. "This old man grew up with the love of his parents and once led an affluent life. He was once as young as you are and had his own interests. But now he is destitute and plagued with sickness. Life is impermanent. The most important thing is that we must show compassionate love and care for each other. These qualities are essential to being a decent human being. Only in this way can we have a peaceful and prosperous life."

The Buddha took every opportunity to teach people. Having heard the Buddha's words, those that were present felt contrite and ashamed. Some of them gave money to the old man, and some helped him up and offered to look after him.

Everyone will go through the stages of birth, aging, illness and death. We cannot dictate or predict what will happen in the future. This is the concept of impermanence that the Buddha wanted to convey to his followers.

The Kin of the Buddha's Previous Lives

Conflict between people is only the continuation of our past anxieties, and it leads to evil consequences in the future.

ne day the Buddha and his disciples were begging for alms. On their way, they met an old man who approached the Buddha with an amicable and reverent attitude. "My son, where have you been for so long? Come, let's go home now. Your mother misses you dearly." The Buddha didn't seem to mind that the old man addressed him this way, and he and his disciples followed the old man home.

On entering the house, the old man called out to his wife, "Come quickly, old lady, I have found our son."

When the old lady saw the Buddha, she greeted him reverently in the manner of a Buddhist. But she also said to him, "My son, where have you been? It's been so long since you left. Do you know how much your father and I have missed you?"

Then she called to her daughter, "Daughter, hurry up and come, your brother has returned."

When the daughter came out, she also said, "Where have you been? We haven't heard from you in ages."

The Buddha acted as if he had indeed come back home and met his own folks. He accepted the meal they provided and then went back to the sangha. All his disciples were puzzled by the incident. "How strange," they thought. "The old man must have known that the Buddha's parents are King Suddhodana and Lady Maya. Why did he call the Buddha his son? Even more strange is that the Buddha seemed to accept this. What is the story behind this?"

Seeing his disciples discussing this matter, the Buddha addressed them. "All of you sit down please. I'll tell you about my relationship with that old couple. It dates a long way back and was formed over a time span of 1,500 eras. During the first five hundred eras they were my parents, during the second five hundred eras they were my uncle and aunt, and during the last five hundred eras they were my grandparents. Because of this special relationship, it is appropriate for them to call me their son. All lives are linked by different causes and affinities. They raised me in my previous lives and are truly my benefactors."

From this story, we can understand that all people meet for a reason. We all come from different backgrounds and there must be a special cause for us to meet and be together. We must cherish that special relationship because it links us together life after life. Whether it is due to a good cause or a bad one, we have all been linked by it from our previous lives until now.

Therefore, we should avoid any arguments with others. Conflict between people is only the continuation of our past anxieties, and it leads to evil consequences in the future. When we understand the concept of "cause, connection, effect and retribution," we will learn to maintain good relationships with people. Only when we appreciate the causes of our past lives and the connection of our present lives will we have the good fortune to meet again in the future.

We should get along well with people both far and near to us, especially those who are by our sides. We must be grateful to them and understand and accommodate them. It is very possible that they were our benefactors in the past. If we were their beneficiaries in the past, we should repay them now. Therefore, in our daily lives, we should always be grateful toward people and events.

The Old Maidservant

We ourselves should give generously and do kind deeds, and we should also urge others to do the same. When we delight in seeing others do good deeds, we will also obtain merits.

n the Buddha's time, there was a venerable elder named Anathapindika who felt the greatest joy when he heard the Buddha lecture. He and his family all became the Buddha's students. They also built an abode for the Buddha and the assembly of monks to live in.

There was an old maidservant in Anathapindika's household who begrudged her master's generous offering to the Buddha. Therefore, every time he and his disciples came to take the meals prepared for them, she became very upset. Once Lady Anathapindika noticed her reaction and said to her, "Do you know that the Buddha is a man of great wisdom? To be able to give to him is our blessing." Nevertheless, the maid still felt that Anathapindika was foolish. She was disturbed whenever she heard the name of the Buddha.

When Queen Mallika heard about the old maidservant's behavior, she called for Anathapindika. "I was told there is a maid in your household who not only disrespects the Buddha, but also speaks scandalously of the Three Treasures [the Buddha, the dharma and the sangha]. Is this true? Why don't you let her go?"

"The Buddha is very compassionate and loves all creatures, but it is not easy to enlighten all people," Anathapindika explained. "Besides, the old woman is poor and lonely. If I fired her, where would she go? Her trouble originates from the bad habits she has accumulated. I want to correct her gradually with love."

"I would like to meet her to find out why she is so disrespectful of the Three Treasures," said the queen.

When Anathapindika returned home, he prepared some gold bars and told the old maidservant to take them to the palace at once. They were for Queen Mallika to give to the Buddha.

The old maidservant was dismayed by her master's instructions. "It's the Buddha again," she thought. "It's bad enough that my master should offer him anything. Now he wants me to deliver this gold to the palace for the queen to give to the Buddha." With such complaints in her mind, she reluctantly took the gold to the queen.

When Queen Mallika received the gold, she softly spoke to the old maid of the joy and emancipation she felt after listening to the Buddha's lectures. However, the maid could neither understand nor accept the queen's appreciation of the Buddha's teachings. Just then, the Buddha came to the palace. As he was being shown in, the maid turned to leave. The queen was able to detain her only after much persuasion.

Since the old maidservant had stayed, she had to listen as the Buddha lectured. The Buddha's benevolent expression and wisdom helped her reach a certain understanding and she felt happy. However, she still steered clear of the Buddha. Whenever he came to Anathapindika's home, she stayed as far away as possible.

"She and I did not get along well in our previous lives," the Buddha explained. "I can't make her trust me. Rahula is the only one who can convert her to Buddhism."

Rahula had only recently had his head shaved. The Buddha asked the adorable young novice to talk to the old maidservant.

Rahula and the old woman had formed a joyful relationship in their previous lives, so when she saw Rahula she was delighted. Rahula imparted to her some of the Buddha's teachings and told her about his life in the assembly. The old maidservant actually listened with great interest and was moved to request to become the Buddha's student. Thus Rahula guided the old maid into the door of Buddhism.

In our daily lives, we ourselves must do good deeds. Moreover, we must urge other people to do the same. When we see others do good deeds, we should feel happy. Anatha-pindika was very happy to give and did his best to set a good example for others. When he saw others delight in learning the Buddha's teachings, he shared their joy. When others had no faith in Buddhism, he felt sorry for their loss. Queen Mallika piously believed in the Buddhist teachings and she hoped that every-one else could learn them too. Therefore, she used her wisdom to help convey Buddhism to the old maidservant. In conclusion, if we want to eliminate obstructions in our lives, we should form and maintain good relationships with other people.

Mind Alone Creates Everything

At the same point in time and under the same circumstances, the mind reacts differently to different events.

imbasara was the king of Magadha in central India. He supported Buddhism and built the Abode of the Bamboo Groove for the Buddha and his disciples to live in.

One day, Bimbasara came to see the Buddha. The king looked tired. Seeing that the king seemed to have aged quickly in a short time, the Buddha was very concerned. "I haven't seen you in a long time. Have the affairs of the kingdom kept you busy?"

The king replied, "Yes, there are so many matters that I must oversee."

After hearing all about the king's current situation, the Buddha asked him to sit down. In order to help relieve the king's tension, the Buddha asked him a hypothetical question. "Suppose one of your attendants rushes in with an urgent report that the great mountain in the east is about to collapse. Shortly after this, guards from the southern border come to

you and say, 'Your highness, the great mountain in the south is about to fall.' Later on,
guards from the western and northern borders
hurry here and make the same reports. Will
you say, 'I'll get back to you on that after I have
dealt with other affairs of state'? Or will you
immediately find some way to stop the mountains from toppling?"

On hearing this, the king's expression darkened and he became very anxious. "Reverend
Buddha, these are grave problems that are
beyond human ability to solve."

"Calm down now," the Buddha continued.
"Think of yourself for a minute. You are getting older and nearing the end of life every
day. Life is impermanent, and old age and
death will soon catch up with you. You are so
busy and tense every day. Have you ever considered what makes you feel happiest and
most at ease?"

The king tried to relax and calmly recall his
past. Then he smiled. "I am most happy and
carefree when I give something to people and
see their expressions of joy and gratitude. Listening to your lectures also gives me immense
joy and peace of mind."

"Indeed," the Buddha said, "it is your own
choice whether you are in a good mood or a
bad mood, busy or relaxed. To be sure the
affairs of the nation are important, but so are

keeping regular hours and a healthy state of mind. Just now, when I asked you to imagine that the great mountains were about to collapse, you immediately became nervous and anxious. At the same time, when you thought of helping and giving to people or listening to my lectures, you smiled and became happy. You see! Mind alone creates everything."

Indeed, at the same point in time and under the same circumstances, we may feel anxious or happy when we have different thoughts on our minds. This is proof that everything is created by the mind alone.

The Clogged Wells

Learning Buddhism all depends on the mind. If we take good care of our minds, then every day is a good day and every deed we do is a good deed.

When the Buddha was alive, he traveled along both sides of the Ganges River teaching his ideas. One day he came to the village of Kusinara, located in central India to the north of the Ganges River. All the people there were Brahmans [believers of orthodox Hinduism]. When they heard about the arrival of the Buddha, they went to each family and warned, "The monk from the Gautama family will be here soon with his students—don't give them any food."

Someone raised a question. "Even without food, they can still survive as long as there is water. Since all our wells are open, they can get water anytime. How can we stop them?"

"Let's seal up all the wells," suggested another. Everyone thought it was a good idea, so they stuffed all the wells with stones, straw and husks.

Having walked for a long time, the Buddha and his disciples rested under a large tree. The Buddha asked Ananda to try to get some water. But Ananda had already heard on the way over that all the wells had been stopped up, so he felt he would not be able to do what the Buddha had asked.

Seeing his disciple's hesitation, the Buddha asked him if there was any problem. "All the villagers here are Brahmans," Ananda said. "When they heard we were coming, they clogged up all the wells. I am afraid I won't be able to get any water."

"Don't worry," the Buddha said. "Where there is a well, there is water. Just do as I say and go fetch some water." Since the Buddha was so sure, Ananda obeyed although he could not figure out what the Buddha had in mind.

Ananda came to an old well, and there he saw something incredible — water was gushing out from the well and the ground was covered with the straw and husks that had been used to stop up the well. Without any difficulty, Ananda filled his bowl with water and went back to give it to the Buddha, who drank one mouthful and found it very tasty. Because the water had been filtered through the straw and husks, it was especially pure and sweet.

"Where did you get the water?" the Buddha asked Ananda. "Didn't you say all the wells had been stopped up?"

"It is truly unbelievable. The water gushed out from the well and washed away all the straw and husks."

"The reason is simple. If the water is there, it is of no use to try to seal it off. In the same way, if we give to people, we will have blessings. When one has no desires, one is self-contained and at ease. On the contrary, if we do not cultivate blessings but keep wanting things, then we suffer from the feeling that we lack something. These Brahmans don't understand the nature of water, yet they want to stop it up. That will never be possible!"

From this story, we can understand the hardship and hostility that the Buddha had to endure in spreading his teachings.

We should know how to work for the well-being of people. Whatever we acquire from nature we must use for nature. The laws of nature must not be violated. Learning Buddhism all depends on the mind. If we take good care of our minds, then every day is a good day, every deed we do is a good deed, and every road is a broad road. If we keep our minds closed, we shall always stumble in darkness.

The Horrible Ghost That Ate People

With purified deeds, words and thoughts and an imperturbable mind, no evil can harm you.

During his travels, the Buddha once came to a small country. At one village in that country, there was a horrible ghost that ate people. Every day at dusk he would appear in the village, and he would eat at least one person a day, sometimes as many as ten or twenty. All the villagers were horrified and wanted to flee to other countries.

The ghost was aware of their intentions. "No matter where you go, I'll find you. Let's make a deal. If you offer me one person a day, I'll leave the rest of you alone that day."

Since there was no place to escape to, the villagers had to accept the deal. From then on, they offered the ghost one person every day. But not knowing when their own turn would come, the people were still constantly worried.

One day it was the turn of the only son of a wealthy, elderly couple. Faced with the fact, the family was engulfed in sorrow. Parents and son hugged each other and wept, but there was nothing they could do except pray sincerely to all the deities.

When the Buddha learned of the situation, he hastened to that village.

The next day, with grave sadness, the couple took their son to the entrance of the cave where the ghost lived. By then, the Buddha had already reached the cave. Since the ghost happened to be out, he went directly into the cave and sat on the ghost's seat in meditation. The son was drawn by the Buddha's kind, dignified visage. He prostrated himself in front of him and then sat down beside him.

Not long after, the ghost came back to the cave. When he saw the dignified, majestic appearance of the Buddha, he was frightened and awed. However, he saw the boy sitting beside the Buddha, so with his magic power he conjured up swords and knives and sent them flying at the Buddha. To his surprise, the swords and knives fell softly to the ground like flower petals. The Buddha sat still, unharmed.

Then the ghost became very angry. He transformed himself into stones and hurtled through the air toward the Buddha. However, the stones landed in front of the Buddha and turned into grains of rice. The ghost was stunned. He realized that the person in front of him must be one of great power and virtue and could never be harmed.

He came to the Buddha and inquired, "Venerable monk, may I ask you what kind of magic you practice that is so powerful?"

"All I have done is to keep my deeds, words and thoughts pure and maintain a serene mind that harbors compassionate love. This is what I have cultivated in myself."

Seeing that the monk possessed great wisdom, the ghost asked, "Would you please tell me what new karma and old karma are?"

"Old karma is generated from ignorance in the past. In your previous life, your deeds were killing, stealing and fornicating; your words were abusive speech, lying, flattery and double-talking; your thoughts were greed, anger and delusion. All of these past thoughts, words and actions created your old karma."

"New karma refers to what you are doing right now. If you can eliminate all evil thoughts, you will not create new karma. All your bad karma will be diminished if you regret your old bad karma and refrain from creating new bad karma."

"What you have said is reasonable," the ghost said. "But I am very hungry right now. Would you please give me the boy?"

"How pitiful you are! Did you know that in your previous life, you were also a monk? But evil thoughts grew in your heart and you created bad karma, so you fell into the Ghost Realm and have been suffering in both body and mind for a long time. Now you still do evil deeds every day. If you continue this way, you will stay forever in the Ghost Realm."

Hearing this, the ghost was so frightened that all his hair stood up. Gradually, his memory came back to him. In his previous life, he had wanted to cultivate himself as a monk. Because he could not rid himself of evil thoughts of killing and fornicating, he had fallen into the Ghost Realm and suffered terribly. He realized that to redeem himself now, he had to resume his spiritual cultivation. Once this good thought entered his mind, the ghost prostrated himself in front of the Buddha and begged him to save him. The Buddha taught him the true Way, and from then on the ghost had no more evil thoughts and abided by the Buddha's teachings.

How powerful the mind is! If you have already created old bad karma and continue to produce new bad karma, how can you ever escape from suffering? Who creates your karma? None other than you yourself. Who can save you? Again, the answer is no one else but yourself. The knot must be untied by the one who tied it. You must examine your actions and correct your mistakes in order to save yourself.

The Miser

*Life is like a field of blessings. If you want to reap
a bountiful harvest, you must cultivate the field with
wisdom.*

In the time of the Buddha, Prensenajit
was the king of Kosala. When he was
young, he was short-tempered and
had no religious beliefs. After he came
to know the Buddha, he frequently listened to
his lectures, and he became a devoted Buddhist
and a great supporter of the sangha.

One evening, the king went to see the Buddha. Noticing that the king was covered with
dust, the Buddha asked him, "What happened?
Why is your body covered with dust?"

"Old man Bhadrika just passed away," Prensenajit replied. "He had no offspring to inherit
his property, so it was turned over to the state
treasury. I went to make an inventory of his
property and the gold bars alone weighed a ton.
Can you imagine the enormity of his wealth?"

"What a pity!" remarked the Buddha.

"Bhadrika was all alone and led a miserable
life. His house was in poor shape, his clothes
were shabby, and he ate sparingly. He lived in
the most frugal fashion, interested only in
guarding his incalculable property. Now he has

left the world and taken nothing with him. Reverend Buddha, with your wisdom, can you see where he went after leaving the Realm of Human Beings?"

"He has fallen into the Screaming Hell. The spirits in this hell wail and scream all the time because of their extreme suffering. That is why it is called the Screaming Hell."

Hearing this, the king sighed. "To come into possession of such wealth, Bhadrika must have had many blessings. Why should he fall into the Screaming Hell in death?"

"He owed his wealth to the blessings he had accumulated in his previous life. Many eras ago, there was a certain landlord. One day, he saw the Pratyeka Buddha begging for alms. On a sudden whim, he gave food to the Buddha and said, 'Any time you are in need of food, I will give it to you.' After a period of time, however, he grew stingy. He regretted what he had promised the Pratyeka Buddha and thought he would rather give the food to his slaves. From then on, he never gave any food to the Pratyeka Buddha."

The Buddha continued, "That landlord was Bhadrika. Because he had given alms to the Pratyeka Buddha when he was a landlord, he accumulated blessings and came into enormous wealth in this life. But because he grew miserly and retracted his promise, he was unable to enjoy what he had in this life. Furthermore, he didn't perform any good deeds or give anything to others during this life, so he fell into the Screaming Hell after his death.

"Are there no blessings left for him? He had such an immense fortune. Couldn't he take some with him?"

"It is like cultivating farmland," the Buddha said. "Suppose all the crops have been harvested. If you don't sow more seeds, can any new crops grow in the field? It is true that Bhadrika was very rich in this life, but he didn't cultivate any new blessings. Naturally, there are no blessings he can take with him."

Only when one has given will one receive. We are rarely born as humans in the cycle of reincarnation, and it is a blessing to be able to give. Life is like a field of blessings in which we can grow anything we wish. How much of the field we cultivate and whether we sow the right seeds in the right season depend on our own wisdom and judgment.

Section 3
A Tragedy Caused by Gluttony

A Tragedy Caused by Gluttony

If you kill an animal to satisfy your desire for good-tasting food, the consequences will make you regret your decision.

igh on a mountain, there once lived a family who made their living by farming and pasturing, and everyone in the family was very frugal. Although each year the crop was abundant and the sheep were well-grazed and sturdy, the family never ate mutton.

When the husband got older, he began to think, "I have raised so many sheep, but I have never once tasted mutton in my entire life. I would sure like to try it some time." He had always taught his children to be frugal and to sell all the crops and animals, keeping nothing for themselves. Therefore he was afraid that if he set a precedent by eating mutton without an appropriate reason, the children would become wasteful. The two thoughts battled in his mind, but his desire for mutton grew stronger each day.

One day, remembering that there was a large tree outside the house, an idea suddenly came to him. "I had a dream last night," he said to his wife. "The tree god told me that we owe our abundant harvests and stout animals to him. He therefore wants us to sacrifice a sheep to him every month."

His family all thought it was reasonable to show their appreciation to the tree god, who might really have been responsible for the large harvests and fat animals. So they started killing a sheep every month as a sacrifice to the deity.

Years later, the husband became sick and bed-ridden. During that time whenever he closed his eyes, he felt as though flocks of sheep were running around inside his head. His painful moans sounded like the bleats of a sheep. What made him suffer most was that he had lied to his family because of his craving for mutton. Although he truly regretted it, no one could understand what he was going through. He died with profound sorrow and a deep sense of guilt.

One night shortly after the funeral, the son dreamed of his father, who said to him sadly, "I lied to you, so now I have fallen into the Realm of Animals." The son woke up surprised, but he did not believe his father's words and dismissed the whole thing as just an insignificant dream.

After the father passed away, the family still continued the practice of sacrificing one sheep a month to the tree god. One day, the son went to the pen to rope a sheep for the sacrifice. But strangely enough, the sheep kept whining and would not budge. The son did not know why the sheep was whining and tugged the rope more forcibly.

At that very moment, a monk went by the place and saw what was happening. He called out to the son. "Young man, stop dragging that sheep. Calm down and think for a while. You must realize that we all have to undergo endless reincarnations and there will be no end to killing if we don't stop now. What do you know? Maybe that sheep was your father!"

The young man was shocked to hear these words. He took a closer look at the sheep and discovered the animal was shedding tears. The sad expression on the sheep's face closely resembled the look he had seen on his deceased father's face in his dream. He hugged the sheep and cried, "Poor father, you have been suffering so!"

We don't know if the father was indeed reborn as that sheep. However, he used the excuse of sacrificing the sheep to the tree god as a way to satisfy his own desire, and he thus lied to his family and planted the bad karma of killing. In the end, he not only brought bad karma and worries to his whole family, but he also suffered by being reborn as a sheep. What a high price he paid! And was it really worth it?

Three Types of Illnesses

If you are obsessed over life and death, all sorts of worries might arise and physical and mental illnesses will appear one after another.

n the Buddha's time, a person called Anathapindika lived in the state of Sravasti in India. A disciple of the Buddha, Anathapindika was a philanthropist famous for his generosity to the needy. He had a very wealthy friend who always felt weak and indisposed. Although he consulted many famous doctors and prayed to many deities, his health still showed no signs of improvement.

When Anathapindika heard about his friend's condition, he went to visit him. "You have been worshipping the deities and have gone to many doctors, but your condition still remains the same. I would suggest you ask the Buddha to visit you. Maybe he can cure your illness."

This friend did not like Buddhism, and he did not understand why Anathapindika supported the Buddha. But Anathapindika knew that his friend was not getting any better and repeated his suggestion on several other occasions. Perceiving his genuine concern for him and in view of their long friendship, the friend finally agreed.

Anathapindika arranged for the Buddha to visit his friend. After the Buddha had examined him, he said to the friend that his illness belonged to one of three types.

The first type of illness is caused when one is sick but does not receive medical treatment. As time passes, a minor sickness becomes a major one. This situation usually takes place in poor families.

The second type of illness arises when one seeks treatment but is not careful in selecting an appropriate remedy. In cases like this, the cause of illness is sometimes psychological, not physical. Patients are so anxious that they consult various physicians, take all kinds of medicine, and pray to deities for a cure. However, if the psychological illness is not cured, the physical symptoms remain.

The third kind of illness is incurred by arrogance and willfulness. People afflicted with this type of sickness indulge themselves in sensuality and materialism and take bad care of their bodies. Furthermore, they are ill-tempered, so when they fall sick they vent their frustration on other people. They have no concept of right or wrong and cannot distinguish between good and evil. Patients like this can be described as beyond redemption. They can only regain health when they wake up and realize the error of their ways.

"When you are sick, you should see the doctor," the Buddha said. "That does not mean that you should be so worried over every little sickness that you see countless doctors and take whatever medicine they prescribe or resort to the gods for help — that would be missing the point. Actually, if you can always be aware of your behavior and reflect on yourself, then your mind and body will be in accordance and no sickness will arise or persist."

"Your sickness belongs to the second type and is nothing serious," the Buddha continued. "So rise and move your body, breathe some fresh air and refresh your mind. Then you can start to develop a healthy body."

After listening to the Buddha's analysis, this person reflected deeply. "That's right! I generally care too much about life and death and I'm too tense, so I take medicine every day and constantly worry. When I really get sick I invoke the deities and worship them, but that never cures me. I've been lying in bed for too long. I really should get out and walk around."

The Buddha smiled. "Aren't you already feeling better now? Both you and Anathapindika are in good health and can vow to do good deeds for others." At that moment, this friend was suddenly awakened and felt very comfortable, both mentally and physically. He immediately asked the Buddha to accept him as his student.

If we look around, we see many people who are troubled by one of these three types of sickness. Therefore, if you are not feeling well, go see a doctor. Don't be overly alarmed by a minor sickness and end up receiving inaccurate diagnoses or the wrong medicine. Furthermore, you must not be superstitious and resort to the gods for help. Abstain from pursuing sensual pleasures and eliminate greed, anger and delusion from your mind. Then your body and mind can be truly considered healthy.

The Bitter Result of Stinginess

You do not have the right to own your life, only the right to use it. You must bear in mind the concept of cause and effect.

In the Buddha's time, there was a very stingy rich man. He was always telling his son to guard the family's wealth and to avoid spending money on inconsequential people or things, because money was not easily made. This rich man went so far as to tell his doorman to drive away any beggar that came to the door and refused to see anyone who came asking for his help. Time went by and this rich man finally died.

Not far away lived a poor family. Both the husband and wife were blind and the pregnant wife was about to have a baby. One day the husband said to his wife reluctantly, "We are poor and can hardly make ends meet. How will we ever be able to raise our child? I think you may be better off if you leave me and find a way to stay alive yourself."

So this poor woman sadly left the house and went begging for a living. After some time, she gave birth to a baby boy who, unfortunately, was also blind. She found a cave in the mountains and settled down there with her baby. She continued to go out and beg for food in the daytime and returned to her baby at nightfall.

When the boy turned seven, he started to go begging with his mother. One day his mother became seriously ill, so she said to him, "Mommy can't go out today, so you will have to beg for food the way I taught you. When you have eaten, don't forget to bring some back for me."

The boy obediently left. When he came to the rich man's house, he sneaked in when the guard was not looking. But it was his bad luck to run right into the rich man's son, now the master of the house. The rich young man was very angry to see a beggar in his home, so he gave the guard a good tongue-lashing. The guard in turn vented his anger on the young beggar by dragging him onto the street and beating him mercilessly with a club. The poor boy was injured badly and bleeding all over.

Someone witnessed the whole incident and ran to inform the beggar's mother. She rushed immediately to the scene and cried bitterly while caressing the boy's injured body. Her wails immediately drew a crowd around her and her son.

At that moment, the Buddha happened to pass by. He saw the boy bleeding in his mother's arms, so he gently rubbed the boy's eyes.

When the boy opened his eyes, he could vaguely see what was around him.

The Buddha asked the boy, "Do you recognize this place?"

The boy felt that the place was very familiar and blurted out, "This is my home!"

"This *was* your home in your previous life. Who were you then?"

The boy sighed as he remembered things from his previous life. "I was the master of this house." At that moment, the rich man's son came out of the house and the Buddha said to the young man, "You are not a very good son."

The young man had no idea what this remark meant. "My father has been dead for seven years. For what reason do you say I am not a good son?"

"Aside from being a bad son, you are also stingy," the Buddha said to him. "Look! Who is this child?"

"I don't know him."

"He was your father. Your father died seven years ago with the bad karma created by his stinginess, so he was reborn into a poor family to suffer the effects. Today instead of giving him something to eat, you drove him away and caused him to be savagely beaten. Think about it and tell me if you were a good son or not."

The rich young man looked at the Buddha's majestic visage and pondered his words. He realized that his father was suffering now because of his miserliness in his previous life.

Do we have the right to own our lives? In truth, nothing but karma remains with us after we die, so we must remember the concept of cause and effect. We must eliminate our evil thoughts and prevent new evil thoughts from arising. If we make a mistake, we must repent at once. Should we fail to do so, we will suffer the consequences and it will be too late to repent then.

Manchai and Sumagadhi

Having the right, broad faith can bring harmony to the whole family. Further extend that faith and every person in society can benefit from it.

There is a story in the *Agama Sutra*. In the state of Sravasti, there was a well-respected elder named Anathapindika who was both wealthy and generous. He had a very good friend named Manchai who lived in a neighboring state. They visited one another regularly and did business together.

One day, Manchai went to visit Anathapindika in Sravasti. Anathapindika introduced his daughter, Sumagadhi, to Manchai. She was beautiful and had all the virtues of a woman. When Manchai saw her, his eyes widened, because he had a son who was old enough to get married. He saw how elegant and virtuous Sumagadhi was and felt she would be a good match for his son. After she left, he said to Anathapindika, "I have a son and you have a daughter. Don't you think a marriage between our two families would be a perfect match?"

Anathapindika replied, "Our backgrounds are very similar and it would be wonderful if your son could marry my daughter — but it is impossible." Manchai asked, "Since our two families are of equal standing and we are close friends, why is it impossible?" Anathapindika replied, "Because we have different faiths."

Manchai asked again, "What is your religion?"

"All my family members are followers of the Buddha," Anathapindika replied. "My daughter holds the Buddha in high esteem and his teachings are an inseparable part of her daily life. But your faith is entirely different from ours. We are good friends, so it does not matter so much that we have different religions. But if my daughter is married into your family, I fear she will find it very hard to get along well with your family."

"We live together but do not have to believe in the same faith," Manchai replied. "She can keep her faith and we will follow ours. Don't worry! She can maintain her Buddhist beliefs."

Anathapindika was touched by Manchai's sincerity, so he agreed to the marriage.

Later, Manchai's family came to Anathapindika's home with an extravagant wedding procession and many treasures. Anathapindika also married off his daughter with a generous dowry.

The wedding entourage returned to their own city, but when they reached the city gate a religious group surrounded them. The city had a law that forbade marriage with outsiders. If anyone broke this law, he or she had to pay a fine of six thousand gold bars and also hold a banquet for six thousand local religious practitioners.

Manchai was aware of the law, so he willingly set up a banquet for these religious people. After that, he also told his son and daughter-in-law to pay their respects to these practitioners. However, these people were used to exposing their upper bodies and were dressed in clothes that left them half-naked.

When the bride heard that they had to dress in that same way in order to pay their respects to these practitioners, she felt it was against her faith and refused to go. No matter how her husband and father-in-law begged her to go, she adamantly refused. This wedding was in the end not so perfect, and Manchai felt very annoyed.

One day, a Brahman scholar came to visit Manchai. When he heard about Manchai's recent dilemma, he said to him, "One time I went to Sravasti and saw the Buddhist sangha, so majestic and orderly. Every one of the monks looked most dignified, and I consider that proof that Buddhism is a fine religion."

"What of it?" Manchai retorted. "We have always believed in our religion and nothing can change that. We can't change our faith simply because we have a daughter-in-law who believes in a different religion."

"What we seek is spiritual faith," the Brahman said. "We should try to go a step further. Like me, I believe in Brahmanism, but I also have much admiration for Buddhism. There's nothing wrong with that."

Manchai thought that what the Brahman said made sense, so he asked his daughter-in-law to come see the scholar. The Brahman then said to her, "Since your religion is so good, why don't you invite the Buddha to come here and speak, so that your father-in-law and your husband can also understand your religion?"

Sumagadhi knew this was a good opportunity, so that evening she went out on her balcony and prayed with utmost sincerity for the Buddha to come to the city.

Back in Sravasti, the Buddha sensed Sumagadhi's prayer and knew that she was in trouble and needed his help. He and his monks immediately set out for Manchai's city.

When the Buddhist sangha arrived, their majesty stirred the hearts of the people. After the Buddha had received a meal, he began his lecture. The news of his speech spread like ripples from Manchai's home through the city to the whole state. It was an event of great impact.

Many people, including Manchai's family, accepted Buddhism. Sumagadhi now lived harmoniously with her husband's family under a shared faith. Having the right faith not only made the whole family happy, but the people of the entire city also benefited from it.

The Inheritance of a Poor Scholar

The best inheritance you can leave to your children is the knowledge that giving is the most joyful thing.

here is a story in a Buddhist sutra. A scholar supported his wife and children by teaching, but since his hometown was poor and he earned a meager salary, he had to leave to teach in a major city in the hope of earning more money.

Twenty years later he had finally saved up some money, and he decided to go home. He traveled with a friend who was also from the same hometown. Their hometown was far off and the journey back took several days. One day during their journey, they came to a little hut. The scholar was very thirsty. "There's a hut ahead of us," he said to his companion. "Why don't we go there and ask for some water?"

When they reached the hut, they heard someone crying inside. They peered inside the hut and saw a woman crying bitterly by a bed, on which a man was lying.

They asked her, "Excuse us, but why are you crying so sadly? Who is that lying on the bed?"

"That is my husband," the woman replied. "He's very sick, but I don't have any money to take him to a doctor. I think I will have to sell myself to raise the money."

The scholar greatly sympathized with the woman when he heard this, so he said to his friend, "Why don't we both take out some money and help her?"

"No way," his friend protested. "You and I have worked hard for the past twenty years to save our money, and now we can finally take it home and help our families. If we give her the money, how are we going to face our families? Your suggestion is totally unacceptable."

The scholar thought his friend had a point. For twenty long years they had toiled hard to save up the money. If they gave the money to this woman, they would be left with nothing and end up just as they had been two decades before. How could they possibly explain that to their families? He couldn't decide what to do.

Then the woman started crying again, and the scholar decided to give her all his money. He said to her, "Use this money to pay the doctor, so that you won't have to sell yourself." The woman was overjoyed and prostrated herself before him in gratitude.

When the scholar and his friend arrived home it was near the end of the year, so everyone was busy doing their New Year's shopping.

The scholar went home hungry, tired and empty-handed. When his wife saw him, she was first full of hope that he had brought home some money so that the children could have new clothes and they could all enjoy a wonderful New Year's meal.

However, crestfallen, the scholar sighed and said to his wife, "Is there anything to eat? I'm starving to death!"

His wife said, "I've been waiting for you to return with some rice! There is nothing at home I can cook."

"I don't care what there is — anything will do," said the hungry husband. The wife realized that her husband was really starving, so she went outside and picked some wild vegetables to cook for him.

She then asked him if anything had happened on his way back, so he told her everything. After hearing his story, she did not blame him but instead praised him for what he had done.

"I am so lucky to be married to a kind person like you," she said. "I'm willing to endure any suffering with you. No matter how poor you are, I will always be with you."

The scholar was truly moved by his wife's words, so both of them praised and bowed to each other. Seeing how noble their parents were, the three children were also deeply touched. "Dad, Mom, don't worry. We'll study hard so you can be proud of us one day." The children did study very hard and were all very successful when they grew up. Following their father's example, they also donated a lot to people in need.

It is a blessing to be able to give to others. The act of giving is the best example parents can set for their children. Parents teach their children by their own conduct and can inspire them to be diligent in their work and willing to help others. It is the best inheritance they can leave them.

Any cause will create a corresponding result. If you do not plant good causes, you will not receive good results. Loving someone else is basic to being a decent human being. If you can donate willingly and unconditionally, you will be joyful and at ease.

Master Ming Hui

With strength and perseverance, you can use your abilities for the good of all people.

 ong ago lived Master Ming Hui, who was virtuous and highly accomplished in his spiritual cultivation. His father died shortly after he was born, and his mother passed away when he was four. His uncle took the orphan in. When he was around eight years old, his uncle decided to send him to be a novice at an old temple in the mountains. But it was a long way to the temple, so his uncle rented a horse and a groom to take him there.

Once on the road, the horse trotted on regardless of the hot weather. Only when they came to a lake did the horse slow down its pace to drink some water. Seeing the animal's tirelessness, the boy realized, "You can achieve your goal only with diligence and hard work."

After many days of travel, they finally reached the temple. Ming Hui was adorable, smart and more mature than the average boy. There was an old monk in the temple who often told him stories from the Buddha's lives when he was cultivating himself as a bodhisattva before attaining buddhahood. One story that made a deep impression on Ming Hui was about when the Buddha was a prince. One day, the prince saw a mother tiger with seven little tigers in the forest, foraging for food. The mother tiger was unsuccessful in her search for food and the cubs were all whining from hunger. The prince felt very sorry for them, so he sacrificed his life for them by making himself their food.

This story really touched Ming Hui, so he was determined that his spiritual cultivation would also incorporate the compassion and courage of self-sacrifice.

He started to meditate on a rock outside the temple to strengthen his courage. One night when he was sixteen years old, he wanted to go deep into the mountains to test his courage. The old monk tried to stop him, but Ming Hui took out a sutra on the Buddha's previous lives and said, "Old master, you often told me the stories about the Buddha's previous lives, and you also encouraged me to have perseverance and fortitude. We all have to die some day. If I can't face death, how can I develop a fearless mind? So would you please let me go?"

Since the old monk had indeed taught him this, he could not stop Ming Hui from going. So the old monk watched silently as Ming Hui went deeper into the mountains.

There were many bears, wolves, tigers and other wild beasts in the mountains. Ming Hui kept telling himself to stay calm and have courage. He continued to walk until he reached a remote area and sat down on a huge rock.

By that time the sun had set. The stars twinkled and the moon glowed in the sky. Ming Hui sat quietly and recited the Buddha's name. Because he was tranquil, every sound he heard, from the calls of insects and animals to the babble of mountain creeks, was clear and beautiful. He could even hear bears and wolves slowly approaching him, but he kept in mind the Buddha's spirit of fearless self-sacrifice and remained very calm. Even when a large black bear trod right by him, he stayed still. In this manner, he sat until daybreak.

When Ming Hui opened his eyes, he saw the shadow of a person some distance away. He looked more carefully and was surprised to see the old monk. The old monk approached him and said kindly, "Have you realized your wish?"

Ming Hui inferred that the old master must have traveled through the night to get there by dawn. He was touched and decided to study with even more diligence to live up to the care and instruction he received from the old master. Later he became a renowned master of the Zen sect.

The point of this story is not to encourage people to sacrifice themselves to the mouths of animals, but to stress that when we recite a sutra, it has to enter our minds and be expressed in the form of daily practice. In this way, we will be able to truly cultivate the strength and courage that are indispensable for us to help and give to people. Then we can go further and use our abilities to serve all people.

Master Genshin

You must polish the mirror of your heart with wisdom and endurance so that it will become clear and bright.

This is a story that took place in Japan. There was once a little boy whose father died when he was very young, so he was raised by his mother. One night, the little boy had a dream. In the dream, he came to a huge temple with a library behind it. In the library were many sutras and mirrors of different sizes, but the surfaces of the mirrors were covered with dust. When the boy saw the mirrors, he thought it would be very nice if he could get one for his mother.

Just as the thought came to his mind, an old monk came to the library and asked the boy, "What are you doing here?"

The boy went to the monk and bowed sincerely. He said, "There are so many mirrors here and I wish to take one back to my mother." The kindly old monk randomly selected a mirror and gave it to the boy, but it was small and dusty. The boy thought, "But it's the big shiny one that I want!" However, he still accepted it respectfully.

The old monk observed his hesitation and asked, "What's the matter?"

The boy replied honestly, "Thank you very much for the mirror, but I really want the big one that can reflect the full length of a person."

The old monk said to him, "This small one is enough. When you have 'nurtured' it until it is larger and the time is right, you can take it to Yokogawa [a place in the Hiei Mountain region in Shiga Prefecture in central Japan] and polish it." Then the monk disappeared.

The boy woke up from the dream and later told his mother about it. "That was an auspicious dream," his mother exclaimed. "Every person has a mirror in his heart. If you polish it often, it will shine. You said you dreamed of Yokogawa. Perhaps it means that you will carry out your spiritual cultivation there in the future."

The boy bore in mind that Yokogawa would be the place to polish his "mirror."

A few days later, the boy and some other children from the same village went to play by a river. There were two rivers there only a short distance apart. One was so clear you could see the riverbed, but the other one was dark and murky.

There was a monk washing his bowl in the dirty river. The boy saw this and thought that this monk was probably from out of town and did not know that there was a clean river nearby, so he called out to him, "Monk, there is a clean river nearby where you can wash your bowl."

The monk noticed how neat and intelligent this boy looked and replied, "Most people tend to make distinctions, but whether the water is clean or dirty makes no difference to me!"

"Is that so?" the boy replied. "But aren't you washing your bowl because it is dirty? In my opinion, a dirty bowl should be washed with clean water for it to become clean. This is probably why I am making a distinction."

When the monk heard the boy's remark, he realized that his own words were inconsistent. He was washing his bowl because it was dirty — that was making a distinction! But then he also said he was not making any distinctions at all! He went to look for the boy.

The boy was counting stones by a river. The monk then asked the boy, "Why are you counting stones? Look, there are any number of stones on the land! Can you count all of them?"

The boy raised his head. "Indeed, I can't count the stones to the last one. But even an infinite number begins with the number one."

When the monk again heard such a wise answer, he knew right away that the boy was a genius and that it would be a waste to leave the boy here in the mountain without giving him a proper education. He asked the boy to take him to his mother. He asked her for permission to take the boy to Hiei Mountain for a proper Buddhist education.

The mother knew that if her son became a Buddhist monk, he could some day contribute a great deal to society, so she agreed to the monk's request. When the monk and the boy reached Hiei Mountain days later, the boy started his education as a young novice and received his Buddhist name, Genshin.

Genshin was intelligent and studied hard. When he was in his twenties, the temple assigned him to give lectures to the ruler of a castle. He was delighted and wrote a letter to his mother, telling her that he was about to give lectures to the ruler. However, his mother wrote back and reproached him. "You are so ignorant! I had hoped you could carry out your spiritual cultivation and nurture your 'heart mirror' to bring benefits to all mankind, but now you are all excited because you can give a lecture to a ruler! How will you accomplish anything this way?"

When Genshin read his mother's letter, he felt ashamed of himself. He decided to further his studies by going to Yokogawa, a region deep inside Hiei Mountain. He studied diligently, and he promoted the Buddhist teachings in the Hiei Mountain area and became one of the greatest Buddhist educators in Japan. Till this day, he is a widely renowned figure.

Each one of us has a mirror in our heart, and to keep it clean and bright we must remember to polish it constantly.

Master Kuya

If you concentrate, you can become sincere. If you are sincere, your wish will be granted. Absolute concentration is powerful enough to overcome anything.

In Japan, there once lived a Buddhist monk named Kuya who loved to travel and chant the name of Amitabha Buddha to teach people about Buddhism. He also paved roads, built bridges, and restored and constructed temples, and so he was highly respected.

One time, a plague spread through Japan. Those who contracted the disease developed a high fever and died. Many who had not contracted the disease also died because they believed they had been infected. People were scared and confused.

Kuya was aware of the widespread panic. So every day he loaded a barrel of sour plum juice and went along the streets calling, "Sour plum juice, sour plum juice! It can cure your sickness and prevent you from getting sick!" Since everyone respected and trusted him, they came out to get some plum juice.

Kuya personally brought the drink to those who believed they were sick and said to them, "You'll feel better after you drink it." And after they drank it, Kuya would tell them, "You are cured." These people then got out of bed and walked around, saying confidently, "I am not and will not be infected!"

To those who really did have the plague, Kuya would say, "Just relax and have faith, and you will recover." He chanted the name of Amitabha Buddha for them and told them to chant it themselves. Some drank the plum juice for four or five days and miraculously recovered.

Kuya's sour plum juice cured many people and contributed greatly to ending the epidemic. Everyone thought it was truly incredible. People would ask Kuya, "Why was your plum juice so effective in treating the plague? Can plum juice really cure diseases?"

Kuya would smile. "It is the panacea for psychological sickness."

People did not understand what he meant and asked him again, "Is it really so wonderful?"

"The drink had no real medical effect. The real remedy was each individual's concentration and faith."

Kuya treated everyone kindly and sincerely, and they reciprocated with trust and respect. He thus established an unshakable image in people's minds. People believed in his words and were induced to have sincere faith.

People who believed they were sick regained confidence and health after drinking the sour plum juice. On the other hand, those who really had the disease received enough liquid to fight the fever by drinking the juice, which also contained elements that helped the body to fight the germs. These patients were also told to have firm faith, so they were able to recover quickly. This testifies to the saying: "If you concentrate, you can become sincere. If you are sincere, your wish will be granted."

Master Tetsuga

Never be shaken by outside praise or criticism.
Those with determination can accomplish anything.

ver three hundred years ago in Japan, there was a monk named Tetsuga (1630–1682) who shaved his head and became a monk at the age of thirteen. He became known throughout Japan for copying the Tripitaka [a Buddhist canon] only after overcoming all sorts of hardship and difficulties.

It was winter in Japan and snow blanketed the capital city. There was a river outside the city with a bridge over it. Aside from those entering the city, few people passed over the bridge. Tetsuga wanted to raise money to carve a copy of the *Tripitaka*, so he often stood by the bridge asking passersby for donations.

Wearing only thin straw clothes, Tetsuga shivered in the blistering cold, but he still called out to passersby, "Please contribute any amount of money you can to help carve the Buddhist canon!" Some people admired his spirit and determination and made donations, but there were also others who despised him or pretended not to see him and quickened their pace as they walked past him.

One day, a samurai and his entourage rode by on their horses. When Tetsuga saw them, he immediately approached them. "I am Tetsuga and I have vowed to carve a copy of the *Tripitaka*. This sutra can purify people's minds and benefit society, so please donate any amount of money you can."

However, the samurai said to him, "Monk, are you out of your mind, standing here in the snow? Copying the *Tripitaka* is a huge project. How do you expect to complete the task single-handedly and by raising money in such small amounts?" The samurai continued to ride forward, but Tetsuga chased after the horse and stopped before the samurai. "I need tens of thousands of pieces of wood to inscribe the canon and now the whole process is about to begin, so please help me!"

"And I thought you had something important to say," the samurai growled impatiently. "It's now very late, so don't block my way. I'm not giving you any money!" He turned and continued riding, and his soldiers even pushed Tetsuga to the ground. The monk got up and started chasing after the group. The horses galloped on, but he also kept after the group. When they reached the city gate, he once again called out to the samurai, "Please help me accomplish this task. Even if you give me one cent, I will be most grateful to you."

"What a stubborn person," the samurai thought. Not able to get rid of Tetsuga, he reluctantly tossed a cent into his collection bowl. But when he turned around to look at the monk, whose face and body were sprinkled with snowflakes, the samurai was stunned: the monk had put his hands together and was bowing deeply to him in appreciation. The samurai was profoundly touched. He felt the monk before him was like a bodhisattva. But to maintain a samurai's dignity, he left without saying a word.

The weather gradually warmed and the snow melted away, causing a great flood that made many people homeless and hungry. Tetsuga was heart-broken to see so many people suffering, so he bought rice with the money he had raised to carve the canon. He told the other monks in his temple to pack the rice into small bags and he personally delivered them to the refugees.

Word spread and more and more refugees came to the temple asking for rice. The monks at the temple had to package so much rice that their hands were all scratched up and bleeding. However, when the monks thought of the many refugees whose lives depended on the rice, they all worked even faster to package more rice. In the end, because there were so many refugees, the money for the canon was all used up.

Once again, Tetsuga had to travel around raising money for the canon. Some praised him for what he had done for the refugees and continued to support him, but there were also others who could not forgive him. They felt he had cheated them by buying rice with the money that was intended for the canon. They insulted him and even threw stones at him and called him a liar. Even so, Tetsuga held firm to his ideal and did not give up.

It took tens of thousands of boards and hundreds of inscribers to carve the *Tripitaka*. The boards had to be made from cherry wood to last longer. In order to help refugees, the work was interrupted several times. As time passed and progress slowed, Tetsuga grew more and more anxious and conducted his fundraising efforts with an added sense of urgency.

When the samurai heard about the monk who put off his project of duplicating a Buddhist canon in order to aid flood victims, he realized that it must be the same one who had tried to raise money from him a few years before. The samurai considered the monk a real bodhisattva, so he vowed to help the monk fulfill his ideal.

The samurai transported ninety thousand cherry wood boards from Nara, in central Japan, to the monk's temple. As soon as the boards arrived, hundreds of craftsmen started working. It took them more than ten years to finish the job. The canon included 1,618 sections and 7,334 volumes. It is said that the canon is now stored in Manfuku Temple in Japan.

Master Tetsuga applied his benevolence, faith and perseverance to accomplish his vow, paying no regard to what people thought of him. As long as we steadfastly hold on to our ideals, know that we are right, and remain diligent, we will be able to attain our goals.

Master Eisai

What brings blessings to people is not a statue of a deity, but someone who actually frees others from their suffering.

Kennin Temple in Kyoto, central Japan, was established in 1202 by Master Eisai (1141-1215). It is the founding place of the Japanese Rinzai Buddhist sect. Master Eisai combined the principles of the Chinese Tientai, Zen and Esoteric sects and created the Japanese Rinzai sect. Eisai became a monk when he was fourteen years old and studied the Tientai and Esoteric sect teachings when he was nineteen. As an assiduous practitioner, he twice went to Tientai Mountain in China to further his understanding of that sect.

On his second trip back from China, his boat had just left shore when the sky suddenly darkened and strong blasts of wind created turbulent waves. Just at that moment, a glistening object surfaced from the sea. When a sailor hauled it onto the boat, they saw that it was a statue of an unknown god. Eisai reverently placed the statue on the bow of the ship and worshipped it. Strangely enough, the sky became clear, the winds abated and the sea was calm again. Everyone on the boat felt a deep sense of reverence toward the statue and joined Eisai in praying to it.

"It's so wonderful that everyone is safe now," Eisai said to them. "I don't know what god this statue represents, but it certainly was finely carved. Besides, the deity is smiling, smiling marks happiness, and happiness is a blessing. So why don't we call it the 'God of Blessing?' I will take it back to Japan for worship."

After his return to Japan, Eisai built the Kennin Temple in Kyoto and placed the statue at the temple gate. He named it "Ebisu" ("God of Blessing") because the statue brought safety and blessings to the people on the boat.

Eisai devoutly revered the God of Blessing. When people came to worship the statue, he also prayed that it would give them blessings.

One day, a man in tattered clothing and with tears all over his face came to pray to the statue. "I am poor and my children haven't eaten in a long time. I could bear it if I were the only one starving, but it breaks my heart to hear my children cry from hunger. So I have come to beg you, the God of Blessing, to grant me good fortune!"

Master Eisai saw the man and asked, "Don't you come here often?"

The man replied, "Yes, I come here at least once a month."

"But your life has not gotten better?"

"No, perhaps I am not praying sincerely enough."

"Is that so?" Master Eisai asked thoughtfully.

"Maybe not, because my prayers always come from my heart. Maybe I've done something wrong. Although I don't think I've ever made any major mistake, I may have made some minor ones unwittingly. That's right, I must have done something wrong for the god to refuse me his blessings."

As Eisai listened, he found the man decent and honest, so he took a gold necklace from the statue to give the man. His disciples were all surprised to see this and asked him, "Master, won't you offend the God of Blessing?"

"No," Eisai replied. "The God of Blessing is like a living bodhisattva, and he is very compassionate. When he faces such an honest, poor man, I think he also wants to help him. So I am giving the necklace on the god's behalf to make life better for this man and his family."

Eisai then presented the necklace to the man. "You can exchange this for some money and buy food for your family." The man was extremely happy and kowtowed repeatedly to thank Eisai.

Eisai's compassionate good deed demonstrates what a true Buddhist should do when facing someone who needs help. He was able to combine the essence of the Buddha's teachings with practical reality, thus reaching a state in which theory and fact coexist harmoniously. For this reason, the Japanese people held him in high esteem.

Actually, the person who brought blessings to people was Eisai, not the statue of the God of Blessing. Eisai was able to help people because he earnestly carried out the Buddha's spirit of compassion through concrete action.

Master Saicho

If you fear no difficulty, there is nothing you cannot do.

Kuo Ching Temple in Tientai Mountain, China, is well known as a sacred site to Buddhists. The temple was the founding place of the Tientai Buddhist sect (or the "Lotus sect") which has had a great influence in both China and Japan.

There was a Japanese monk named Saicho (767–822) who vowed to promulgate the Tientai sect philosophy in Japan. He became a monk when he was thirteen years old. With exceptional intellectual powers, he read and comprehended all the Buddhist scriptures in his temple. The Chinese monk he most admired was Master Chien Chen (687–763) who had been invited by Japanese monks and the Japanese emperor to visit Japan. Chien Chen felt that Japan had a deep affinity with Buddhism, so he sailed to Japan to propagate the Buddhist teachings. Even after many shipwrecks and the loss of his eyesight, Chien Chen was unshaken in his determination to go to Japan. He finally reached that country and the emperor bestowed on him the title of "Great Dharma Master of Transmitting the Light."

Inspired by Chien Chen's perseverance, Saicho decided to visit China.

At that time, travelers had to go by sea from Japan to China. No one knew what dangers awaited them on the unpredictable ocean.

Not long after Saicho departed from Japan, their boat met with strong winds and turned back to Japan. Saicho and his students had to take another boat. However, when this boat reached the island of Kyushu in southern Japan, it was grounded by a tempest. They were stranded in Kyushu for several months.

While on shore, Saicho took the time to carve a statue of the Buddha. When the boat set out again, he boarded with the statue and continued carving. However, they ran into another typhoon that caused the boat to pitch and toss violently. The people on the boat were horrified and did not know what to do.

Then someone said, "Isn't there a monk on the boat who is carving a statue of the Buddha? Can he come and pray for us?" Saicho appeared and said to them, "My prayer alone is not powerful enough—we must all pray together."

All of the people wanted to live, so they prayed devoutly together with Saicho. Miraculously, the winds soon subsided and the sea was calm again. But the sails and the oars had been destroyed, so the boat drifted where the wind blew. Everyone aboard endured hunger and thirst until they finally reached land more than fifty days later.

Saicho fell sick and did not recover for half a month. Afterwards, he and his disciples traveled for days and underwent all sorts of difficulties until they finally reached Tientai Mountain.

During his stay at Tientai, Saicho diligently studied the Chinese language and was thus able to comprehend the subtle teachings contained in the obscure Chinese Buddhist texts. His mentor was very impressed by his diligence and dedication.

"More than two hundred years ago, Master Tientai [or Master Chih Yi, founder of the Tientai sect] predicted on his deathbed that the Tientai philosophies would spread to the east," his mentor told Saicho. "Now you have come here from Japan and are studying with such concentration. You will be the one who introduces the Tientai teachings to Japan. Therefore, you must study even further."

His mentor brought him to the library in the temple. "I really would like to show you all the great Tientai scriptures," his mentor said, "but unfortunately the key to the library door has been lost. This library has not been opened for two hundred years." When Saicho heard this, he immediately took out a key from his pocket. "Can we try to open the door with this key?" Sure enough, that key opened the door.

His mentor was overwhelmed. "Where did you get this key?"

"I used to study on Hiei Mountain in Japan. The temple once underwent extensive expansion and I found this key on the ground near the construction site. For some reason I picked it up and have been carrying it with me ever since."

"So you *are* the one who was destined to bring the Tientai philosophy back to Japan," his mentor marveled. "How extraordinary! Master Tientai's prediction has finally come true!"

Later Saicho did indeed propagate the Tientai philosophy in Japan. He became the founder of the Japanese Tientai sect and taught on Hiei Mountain.

Saicho's accomplishment was the result of combined confidence, persistence and courage. It shows that if you do not fear any difficulty, you will eventually complete any task you undertake and good fortune will always be on your side.

Section 4
The Animals Show Gratitude

The Animals Show Gratitude

All living creatures have the buddha-nature with-in them. Even animals are capable of feeling sincere gratitude.

One day, a group of monks were discussing ways to carry out spiritual cultivation. "In a Brahman congregation, there is one Brahman who is very devoted to serving others," one monk said to the others. "He willingly prepares food for five hundred Brahmans and also keeps their training ground neat and tidy. Therefore, the other Brahmans can carry out their spiritual cultivation without worrying about anything else." The other monks all agreed that the spirit of this Brahman was very admirable.

Then the Buddha approached the monks and asked, "What are you all talking about?" After they had prostrated themselves before the Buddha, they told the Buddha about the Brahman.

When the Buddha heard about the Brahman, he smiled and said to them, "Do you know what? He has been serving others ever since his previous life."

The Buddha then told them a story about this Brahman. In his past life, he carried out his spiritual cultivation on a mountain. Once there was a drought, and the rivers and creeks all dried up. The animals on the mountain had no water to drink and were dying of thirst. So, every day this practitioner went down the mountain to a river far away. There he used hollow bamboo stems to collect water, which he brought back to the mountain for the animals to drink.

However, as he went back and forth fetching water every day, he neglected his own health and grew weaker and weaker. Still, he mustered up what little energy he had and continued serving the animals.

The animals were grateful to this practitioner but worried about his health. They gathered one day to discuss how they could repay his kindness.

"We don't have much strength, but we can still do what we can to help him," the lion said. "If you can climb trees, go pick fruit for him. If you can't fly, look for food on the ground..."

In order to repay his kindness, all the animals tried their best to find food. Birds came back with small fruits, rabbits found carrots, squirrels brought nuts, horses gathered edible leaves, and so on. When the practitioner saw their efforts, he was deeply touched and real-

ized that all living creatures had an innate buddha-nature. Even animals feel gratitude.

"Giving is not just about giving material
goods," the Buddha told the monks. "If you
serve all living beings with a joyous heart, that
is also giving." This practitioner could serve so
many people and animals because he had love
and persistence. His was spiritual cultivation of
an extraordinary kind.

If every person can give to others with gratitude, our world will be a pure and peaceful
place. If everyone can respect and care about
one another, our society will be filled with
brightness and warmth.

The Monk and the Fox

If you abide by the precepts, you can keep yourself from making mistakes and doing evil. If you compose yourself through meditation, you will have no doubts in your mind. If you have wisdom, you can tell right from wrong.

A long, long time ago, there was an old monk and a novice living in a temple in a small Japanese village. The monk enjoyed playing Japanese chess and lost track of time each time he played. One day, the monk was asked to perform funeral services for someone who had died in a neighboring village. But the old monk was in the middle of a chess game, so he told the person who had been sent to fetch him, "I'll go as soon as I finish this game." But then he kept playing one game after another. It was already late in the afternoon when he finally set out for the neighboring village.

By the time the funeral service was over, it had already become dark. The master of the bereaved family invited the monk to stay for the night, because the monk would have to pass through a forest and over a mountain to get back to the temple, and it would be dangerous to travel in the dark. However, the monk thought, "The novice is all alone in the temple. If I don't go back now, he will be afraid." So he declined the invitation but accepted some food and money prepared by the bereaved family. Then the old monk hurried home.

As he was passing through the forest, he suddenly heard a noise behind him. He turned around to find a skinny dog. The old monk tried to shoo it away, but the dog did not leave. Instead, it stood there and looked right at the monk. Since the old monk had to be on his way, he continued walking with the dog following behind.

The monk came to a village and he stopped to ask some children, "Do any of you know whose dog this is? " No one knew where the dog came from, so the monk continued walking and the dog continued trailing behind him. Gradually the sky grew darker and it became hard to see the road ahead.

The monk knew there was a little hill ahead and he would need a lamp to cross it. So he went into a store to borrow a lamp. However, he felt it would be impolite to borrow something from the shopkeeper without making a purchase, so he asked her if they had any rice cakes left. She replied, "We just happen to have five left." The monk asked her to wrap all five of them and then asked to borrow a lamp. The shopkeeper found a lamp and placed a candle inside it.

The monk again inquired, "Do you know anyone around here who owns a dog?" She replied, "Not that I know of, but I've heard that on the road you just came from there is a fox that often uses its magical powers to trick people." Hearing this, the monk became suspicious. As he set out again with the cakes in one hand and the lamp in the other, the dog still trailed behind him. Recalling what the shopkeeper had said, the monk suspected that the dog was really the fox. He became very frightened and quickened his pace.

As he walked on, he suddenly discovered that all the cakes had disappeared! Could the fox have stolen them? Overwhelmed, the old monk began to run. When he finally arrived at the temple gate, he immediately called out the novice's name, "Ching Kuan, Ching Kuan!" The novice rushed out and opened the door. The monk turned around to see the dog still behind him, so he said, "Quick, get the broom! There's a fox behind me!"

The novice got out the broom but said, "Look, the dog is holding something in his mouth." When the monk took a closer look, he noticed that they were the lost cakes. He told the novice, "Get them, quickly!" The novice casually approached the dog and patted its head with one hand while retrieving the cakes with the other hand. The monk was quite surprised. "That's a fox you're patting! Aren't you afraid?" The novice replied, "But he's behaving very well! He doesn't seem like a fox to me." Still doubtful, the monk had the novice drive the dog away with the broom.

After the dog had gone, the monk regained his composure and asked the novice, "When I was calling for you to open the gate, did you come down from the bell tower?" The novice replied, "Yes, because I was so bored all by myself." The monk asked him, "Then you didn't feel bored when you were in the tower?" "No," the novice replied. "I struck the bell and the chimes sounded like you talking to me, so I was able to remain calm."

The monk was stunned. He turned around to see if the dog was still around, but it had already left. "Quick! That was a dog, not a fox! He was probably so skinny because he hadn't eaten for days. Yet when I dropped my cakes on the ground, he brought them back to me without taking a single bite. The poor dog! He must be starving! Find him quickly!"

The monk regretted that he had been so easily influenced by what the shopkeeper had said, which made him lose his good sense and mistake the dog for a fox. The young novice was in the temple alone, but he was still smart enough to strike the bell and make like the old monk was talking to him. The young novice's simplicity and wisdom made the monk feel ashamed of himself. As he reflected on his recent behavior, he realized that he should constantly bear the Buddha's teachings in mind and observe the precepts, practice meditation and thus develop wisdom. Then he would never become unduly suspicious when confronted with events in life.

There are three aspects in learning Buddhism — the precepts, meditation and wisdom. When we abide by the precepts, we can prevent ourselves from making mistakes and doing evil. When we compose ourselves through meditation, no confusion will arise in our minds. When we have developed wisdom, we can tell right from wrong. The young novice had wisdom that was pure and unsophisticated. The skinny dog knew his place and was not greedy. As for the honest monk, he also had the courage to admit and repent of his mistake, and when one repents one is purged immediately. Thus, even in the quiet mountain village, a pure stream of Buddhist wisdom flowed.

The Greedy Little Leopard

If you can eliminate greed and lead a simple life, you will be free from the worries that arise from trying to satisfy your greed.

he Buddha once told his disciples a story. In the wilderness, a little leopard left his group to go searching for food. However, he was unsuccessful and was soon hungry.

Suddenly, he found an elephant lying on the ground. He approached it and discovered that it was dead. Delighted, he took a bite at the elephant's trunk, but it was as hard as wood. So he bit at the elephant's ear, but it was like biting on a piece of metal! He chewed on the elephant's tail, but it was also as hard as wire.

By this time the little leopard was truly starving, so he circled round and round the elephant, hoping to find a place to start eating. He finally found that the elephant's belly was soft. He bit deeper and deeper and thus worked his way into the elephant's belly.

The little leopard stayed inside the elephant's body, where there were many internal organs for him to feast on. When he was full, he fell asleep. When he woke up, he resumed eating.

A few days later, scorched by the sun and dried by the hot wind, the elephant's skin shrank and the hole by which the little leopard had entered also tightened. Discovering that the space around him was getting smaller and darker, he grew anxious and tried very hard to break through the skin, but it was to no avail.

Then one day it rained and the corpse became swollen and rotten. With all his might, the leopard finally broke out from the great beast.

He cried happily, "The world outside is so big and free!" However, he immediately discovered that he was very weak and had no hair at all, because he had been struggling so hard inside the belly and had been soaked in filthy blood for days. With all his hair gone, he looked like a freak.

The little leopard bitterly regretted having left the vast, broad world, which he should have appreciated more, for the filthy world of the elephant's bowels. And when he finally made his way out, he realized that he was not himself anymore.

"Ordinary people have greedy thoughts just like this little leopard," the Buddha told the monks. "Once greed takes over, you depart from the pure world and fall into a world of filth that is difficult to escape from. So, each of you must look after your mind and see that greed does not possess it, lest you hurt yourself or other people."

If you can eliminate greed and lead a simple life, you will be free from the worries that arise from trying to satisfy your greed and thus lead a pure, stable life.

The True Hometown

Life is full of truths and falsehoods. With true wisdom, you can learn from disputes over what is true and what is not.

During the Warring States period (403–222 bc) in ancient China, there was a man who was born in the northern state of Yen but grew up in the state of Chu, in central China. As he got older, he thought more and more about returning to his birthplace and spending the rest of his life there. Around that time, a friend of his happened to be going to Yen on business, so they traveled together.

The man had never gone far from home, while his friend was a businessman who traveled constantly between Yen and Chu. Several days later they arrived at a certain place. "We have arrived in Yen," his friend told him. "Your hometown is not far off." After walking awhile, they saw some ruins, and his friend said, "Look, that is your family's ancestral temple." This man was saddened when he observed the dilapidated condition of the temple.

Later when they arrived at a deserted place, his friend said, "Here lie your parents and ancestors." The man was overwhelmed by emotion when he saw the graves, and he started to cry uncontrollably. Seeing him in this state, his friend burst out laughing.

"For decades I have held fond memories of my hometown," the man angrily said. "Now I have seen how places that mean so much to me have been reduced to ruins and buried in weeds. I am extremely upset. How can you be so happy?"

"I was only kidding," his friend said. "It's still a long way to Yen!" Once the man heard his friend say this, his sadness evaporated and he thought, "This is not my real hometown, so how come I cried so bitterly?"

They continued walking and arrived in Yen days later. There he was able to see his ancestral temple and the graves of his parents and ancestors. However, this time he had no special feelings. He simply paid his respects and contemplated the relics in silence. He had realized that in life there were so many things that seemed true yet were false, and vice versa. One reacted in fact to one's own moods and thoughts, not necessarily to reality.

In this story, the nostalgic man did not ascertain whether or not the places that his friend pointed out to him were indeed the actual locations of his ancestral temple and graveyard, but simply reacted emotionally to whatever his friend told him.

Isn't it true that we often encounter similar situations in daily life? We make mountains out of molehills and agonize over meaning-less matters. If we can distance ourselves and calm down to think things over carefully, we will discover that we are simply bringing troubles to ourselves.

The mind alone creates everything. If we can observe the essence of everything around us and fully comprehend what is true, then we will realize that there is actually nothing worth getting agitated about and there is no need for us to feel greed and anger or to have delusions. Although there will always be dis-putes as to whether things are true or false, we can always learn something from them, and that is true wisdom.

It is very simple to let go of our worries. A simple change of attitude will enable us to open our minds and free ourselves from worrying over the different situations we face in life.

The Large Tree

With due reflection and earnest practice, you will be able to apply the Buddha's teachings in your daily life.

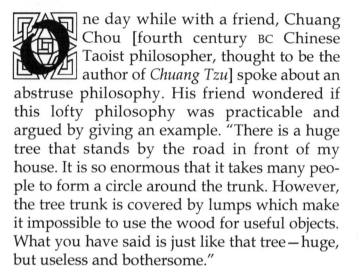 ne day while with a friend, Chuang Chou [fourth century BC Chinese Taoist philosopher, thought to be the author of *Chuang Tzu*] spoke about an abstruse philosophy. His friend wondered if this lofty philosophy was practicable and argued by giving an example. "There is a huge tree that stands by the road in front of my house. It is so enormous that it takes many people to form a circle around the trunk. However, the tree trunk is covered by lumps which make it impossible to use the wood for useful objects. What you have said is just like that tree — huge, but useless and bothersome."

"Actually, you don't need to worry about the tree," Chuang Chou replied. "If you move the tree to the more spacious countryside, it will provide shade from the sun where people can cool off and relax. This way the tree won't have to be cut down and it can still be useful."

Many people tend to think of Buddhism as too profound to be applied in their daily lives.

In truth, if you know how to practice the theories, even a few short phrases will become immensely helpful. But how can you understand the essence of Buddhism and apply it to daily life? You must expand your mind to absorb the Buddhist teachings, contemplate their meaning and practice them in earnest.

The Gourð

*"I was created for a reason." Every person born
into this world is gifted with his or her special powers.*

One day, Chuang Chou's friend Hui
Shih told him, "Emperor Hui of the
state of Wei gave me the seed of a
large gourd. I planted the seed and
indeed it produced a large gourd, so big that
it could hold about five hundred pounds of
rice. But the gourd could not be used to hold
water for it was not hard enough. So I cut it in
half to make two ladles. However, the base
was too wide and the depth too shallow, so it
couldn't hold much and was inconvenient to
use. I became so frustrated that I smashed it
on the ground."

"That's too bad," Chuang Chou said with
regret. "If it could not hold water, you could
have woven a net to hold the gourd and tie it to
your waistband, then you could float in the
water with no effort at all. How joyous and free
you could have felt! If you had known how to
use it, the gourd could have been a very good
tool. Too bad you didn't know how to use it
and ended up destroying it."

Chuang Chou's words are also applicable to humans: people all have strengths and weaknesses and we have to know what our strengths are. Every person born into this world is gifted with his or her peculiar powers. We should use these powers as best we can to serve others, so as to make the fullest use of our lives. The most useful life can be lived only when you truly understand yourself. "To know others, know yourself first." If we try to understand others before we understand ourselves, we will get our priorities wrong and suffer much confusion. If we want to know ourselves, we must remember to reflect often upon our inner world.

The Fish That Sought Help

The value of doing good deeds lies in our sincerity and our knowledge of how much we can do and when we should help, without imposing on ourselves or others.

There is a story in *Chuang Tzu*. A man named Chung Chou was very poor and never had any food in his house. One day he went to borrow some rice from a friend. "I'd be happy to give you some," the friend said. "But I don't have very much rice at home now. Please wait for me to collect the rent from the tenant farmers, and then I'll lend you three hundred gold pieces."

Chung Chou was very displeased to hear this. "On my way to your home yesterday, I heard a voice calling out to me for help. I turned around and saw a fish trapped in a wheel rut on the road. The fish asked me to get some water to save it.

"So I said to the fish, 'I'll go to the kings of the states of Wu and Yueh in the south and ask them to divert water here from the far-off Hsi River so that you may return to the East China Sea. Is that all right with you?'

"The fish was very angry. 'I have no water, which I need to live. All I ask for is a life-saving bucket of water. How could you give me an answer like this? You might sooner go to a fish market and find me there! By the time you channel the water from the Hsi River, I will have become a dried fish!'"

Having finished this story, Chung Chou left.

He lived an extremely hard life and his most urgent problem was that he had no rice to eat. All he needed was some rice to fill his stomach. He was not asking for more than he needed, and he could not possibly wait for the gold promised for some distant time.

There is a saying: "If you want to save a life, you must do so right away." This is what Chung Chou conveyed through his fable of the fish. The fish was dying, and if it waited too long it would die. No matter how much water was given to it afterwards, it still wouldn't save its life!

Sometimes, all people need is a cup of water, a smile, or a helping hand. If we can give in time, we will be happy and the recipient will certainly be grateful. If we are reluctant to give, or if we wait until we are more wealthy or capable, oftentimes we will miss the crucial moment.

The Buddha said, "Refrain from all bad things, do all good deeds." The value of doing good deeds lies in our sincerity and our knowledge of how much we can do and when we should help, without imposing on ourselves or others. In learning Buddhism, we learn about the simplicity and straightforwardness of life and earnestly practice the Buddha's teachings. Only by making Buddhism a part of our lives will we be able to realize the spirit of kindness, compassion, joy and unselfish giving, and do good for all people.

In sum, when we do good deeds, we must do so in a timely manner. We should not miss any opportunity to do good. Nor should we neglect to do something because we think it is insignificant or procrastinate in extending a helping hand to those urgently in need. "Do not neglect a good deed because you think it is insignificant; do not commit a bad deed because you think it is unimportant." By giving out timely love and caring for and helping others, we can create a beautiful and blissful life.

Smart, Kind, Young Taroo

The measure of happiness is not material wealth. Love and good thoughts are what make people happy and content.

bout two hundred years ago in Japan, there was a little village where mostly poor tenant farmers lived. In one family, there lived a husband and wife and the husband's old mother. The couple was very good to the mother and worked very hard. At sunrise, they went out to work. At sunset, they came home and rested. Although poor, the family lived each day in happy contentment.

After some time, the young wife gave birth to a baby boy. But because she was chronically malnourished and lost too much blood after giving birth, she grew weaker and weaker and finally died three months later. The baby she left behind was named Taroo.

The little boy had no idea that his mother had died, and he cried loudly with hunger.

The grandmother nestled Taroo in her arms as she worried about how to feed him. Fortunately, because this family had always treated people with kindness, the neighbors were happy to help them with feeding the newborn.

As the days went by, young Taroo grew to be an adorable boy and he brought his father and grandmother much joy. The father worked in the field and also delivered goods to the city.

One day when Taroo was six years old, he heard a horse neighing outside, so he ran to the stable, stood on his toes and patted the horse's back. "You are going to the city today," he said to the horse. "How I wish I could go too!"

At that moment, his father came in. "Did you tell the horse you wanted to go to town too? What did the horse say?"

Taroo replied with quick wit, "He said yes!"

"Well then," the father said, "let's go together."

So that day young Taroo went to the city with his father. After having delivered the goods, his father asked him, "Do you want anything to eat?"

Taroo said with precocious understanding, "I don't want anything, but I would like to get some of the candy that Grandma likes!" And so they did.

"You can also buy something for yourself," his father said. Taroo picked out a small flute, the cheapest musical instrument. He put the candy in his pocket and played the flute happily.

The sun was setting when they set out toward home. Riding on the horse, Taroo saw flocks of sparrows flying by with rosy clouds in the background. It was a beautiful scene, and Taroo said, "Look how free the birds are, and how radiant the red sun is!"

The father said, "Yes, it's a very beautiful world."

After walking for a distance, Taroo suddenly called out and reined in the horse. "Dad, look! There's a sparrow on the road. It seems to have gotten separated from his flock!"

There was indeed a sparrow on the road. It was eating the rice grains some farmers had dropped on the road and it was paying no attention to anything else. If the horse had taken one more step, the bird would have been killed.

Taroo called out to the bird, "Little sparrow, leave now! Hurry and leave!"

Finally, the bird flapped its wings and flew away. The father was very happy to see what a smart, kind boy Taroo had grown into.

When they arrived home, the grandmother came out from the house immediately because she had heard the clattering of the horseshoes. Although the house was old and bare, their wonderful love and good thoughts filled their lives with blessings and warmth.

It is evident from this story that money is not the line that separates the happy from the unhappy. The most important thing is having love and good thoughts. With sincere love, you can live happily and contentedly despite lack of material wealth.

The Old Man Who Sought the Buddha's Teachings

The meaning of life lies not in its length, but in what we make of it.

Time goes on ceaselessly and every moment we get older and older. Life is constantly generated and exhausted in the cycle of reincarnation. Therefore, we must use our time wisely and do something meaningful.

The meaning of life lies not in its length, but in what we make of it. So what standards do we use to measure the value of life?

The Buddha was once lecturing in Magadha, a state in central India. One day, an emaciated old man with a hunched back came to the gate of the lecture hall and asked to see him. However, he was stopped at the gate and told, "The Buddha is giving a lecture right now, you shouldn't go in there and interrupt him." But this old man kept kowtowing and begging, hoping to see him as soon as possible.

The Buddha knew that something was going on outside, so he said to one student, "Go and

see. If someone wants to come in, ask him in."
Thus the student went and came back with the
old man.

When the old man was led before the Buddha, he prostrated himself and kowtowed with
tears drenching his face. "I am so delighted to
finally be able to see you! I am so old but I cannot die! What evil have I done? Why am I so
wretched? Buddha, what I most hope for now is
to become your disciple and monk. This is my
only wish in life."

"It's very good that you have this wish," the
Buddha said to him. "The duration of life is not
important. What is important is the mind. Life
exists because of karma. Everyone is born in
this world with his own karma and united with
parents who were somehow related to him in
past lives. How long you live and how much
wealth you have are also determined by the
karma created in your past lives."

Then the old man asked the Buddha, "What
bad karma did I create in the past?"

"In the past, you fawned on the rich and bul-
lied the poor. You had no compassion, and you
were cruel and greedy..." The Buddha went on
to enumerate many wrongs that the old man
had committed in the past. For example, he
never sympathized with people who were suffering or admonished himself not to be like
those who committed bad deeds.

"Such terrible causes," the old man said. "I can't believe I created so much bad karma! So that is why I have suffered so much torment in this life." He repented before the Buddha in the hope of speedy emancipation from all his suffering in this lifetime.

"I am willing to accept all the consequences of my past bad deeds," he then said to the Buddha. "Now I beg you to accept me as your disciple and give me the chance to practice all the precepts." The Buddha smiled and said benevolently, "Your wish is granted. Your heart is pure at this moment and now is the time for you to become a monk and practice all that I am going to teach you."

The old man was overjoyed that the Buddha was willing to accept him as a new disciple and even allow him to follow him and practice all his teachings. This was the happiest and most meaningful moment of the old man's life. He knew that being born human was a rare fortune and that the Buddha's teachings were not easily heard, so he felt very blessed to be able to hear the Buddha's teachings and have the chance to practice them.

Section 5
The Young Man
and the Five Turtles

The Young Man and the Five Turtles

Different attitudes toward life cause people to have different values. It is more valuable to have the right attitude toward life than to have great wealth.

There was once a loving father and a good son who were poor but happy. They had a small piece of farmland which they faithfully sowed and plowed. Father and son made a modest living by selling their crops. After many years of frugal living, they gradually saved up some money. One day, the father told his son, "You have had a tough life since you were young. I am so sorry that I never gave you a comfortable life."

"No," the son replied considerately. "It is my fault that I cannot earn more money to provide for you in your old age. It is I who should apologize."

"Although our life is hard, our minds are peaceful," the father then said. "We have saved some money, so we ought to make good use of it. Small as our farm is, it is really difficult for us to plow it by ourselves. I want to buy an ox to help with the plowing."

He gave his son the money and said, "Take this money into town to buy an ox." The son also thought it was a reasonable idea to buy an ox. His father was old and feeble, and an ox would relieve his father of the hard labor.

He took the money and said, "All right, don't worry, I'll be back soon." "The town is a long way off," the father warned. "Take care not to lose the money. It is the reward of our many years of efforts." The son promised to be careful and left.

He traveled across land and water and was quite tired by the time he reached a river. Sitting on a rock, he ate the lunch his father had prepared for him and thought, "How am I going to cross such a huge river?"

While he was staring at the river, he heard children laughing. He followed the sound and spotted some five or six children in the distance. Walking towards them, he saw that they seemed to be hitting some rocks with ropes and rods. On closer inspection, he discovered that the stones were actually a big turtle and four small ones. These children had turned the turtles upside-down and whirled them on their backs. To protect themselves, the turtles had tucked their heads and legs into their shells. However, the children were trying to force the turtles to stretch their heads out by hitting them with ropes and sticks.

The young man felt sorry for the turtles. "Why are you torturing these turtles? They are also living beings that can feel terror and pain. Why don't you put them back into the river?"

The children turned to look at the young man. "What do you know, anyway? It took us a long time to catch the mother and baby turtles. It's none of your business what we do with them."

They again started to deliberately torture the turtles. "Everyone has parents and children, just like the mother turtle and little turtles," the young man said. "Children feel heartbroken at seeing their parents hurt, and parents also feel pain at seeing their children suffer. It is absolutely wrong for you to torture the mother and babies."

Despite the young man's exhortations, the children tortured the turtles even more severely. One older boy even said he would string the turtles together one by one with a rope.

The young man could not tolerate their behavior and asked, "What will you do with these turtles?"

"Sell them for money!"

"How much do you want for the turtles?" the young man asked. The children quoted a large sum. "The man touched the money in the bag on his waist and thought: "Father gave me this money to buy an ox. If I give it to them, I cannot buy the ox." But the children had strung up the turtles and were swinging them from side to side. The young man felt immensely sorry for them, so he resolutely unfastened the bag. "I only have so much money. Give me the turtles in exchange for the money." So the children took the money and put the turtles down.

After the children had left, the young man unfastened the rope, brought the turtles to the riverbank one by one, and said to them, "Now you are free and have no need to be afraid anymore. You can swim freely in the river. Go!" However, the five turtles refused to leave and raised their heads to look at the young man.

"Go on," the young man said again. "If you stay here and those naughty children come back, you'll be tortured again. Hurry and go!" But the turtles just stayed there and stared at him. He said, "I spent so much money because I wanted to see you safely swimming in the river. Don't make me worry about you. Go on!"

As though they understood his words, the five turtles swam into the river. Even in midstream, they kept turning back to look at the young man. The young man waved goodbye to them, and they finally swam off. The young man felt very happy for the turtles — but what about the ox? He now had no money, and he had no other choice but to go home empty-handed.

When he recounted what had happened to his father, the old man smiled and patted him on the head. "Well done! We can always save up more money if we work hard, but five lives would have been lost forever if you hadn't saved them. You made better use of the money by saving five lives than by buying an ox. I'm really proud of you!" Both father and son felt peaceful and content.

That night while sleeping, they heard someone knocking at the door. When the father opened the door, he saw an ox with a note hung around its neck which read, "To show their gratitude, the turtles collected gold nuggets on the riverbank with their mouths and bought an ox as a gift for their benefactor."

The story itself may seem incredible, but the message it carries is the truth. Poor as the father and son were, they respected all living creatures. What noble people! Their attitudes toward life and views on money were quite different from those of the rude children who squandered their time and had no respect for other creatures.

The Buddha wanted us to cultivate our goodwill and do good deeds at all times. Therefore, we must fine-tune our attitudes and avoid improper behavior.

A Carefree Old Man

Worry contaminates our nature. If we face the world with our pure nature, we can then make full use of our lives.

Not long ago, an old man who was a hundred and one years old came to the Abode of Still Thoughts. He looked quite robust, with his straight back and agile gait. When he was hospitalized in the Tzu Chi General Hospital not long ago, our volunteers talked to him about Tzu Chi. He was moved by what he heard and felt happy to have had the chance to learn about us. The volunteers also told the old man about me, so he was determined to come see me. When he came, he conversed fluently with me.

His grandson said to me, "Grandpa can even help us with some simple household chores." I asked the old man, "What can you do for your grandson?" He answered, "I can sweep the floor, wipe tables and fold the clothes." His grandson added, "Grandpa even washes his own clothes!" How impressive it is that he can still do his own laundry and act so nimbly at his ripe old age.

He said, "I am really glad to have met you today, Master." Holding my hands, he repeatedly told me how happy he was. I gave him a string of Buddhist beads and he put them on his wrist. He kept feeling the beads and said, "I am happier now than if I had received two million dollars! I have earned so much today!"

When I gave him my blessings to take refuge in Buddhism, he said, "Wow! It is just as though I had been given five million dollars today! I'm really happy!" I could tell that his happiness was heartfelt. He told me that he had been born during the Japanese occupation of Taiwan and life then was hard. He was illiterate and had done much heavy labor. Toughened by the hard times, he never dared to be idle and he lived every day of his life in earnest. What a fulfilling one hundred and one years he has lived!

He said, "Because I can't read, I never have worries that come from knowing too much—I simply do whatever I have to do." Actually, leading a productive life free from worries is quite an achievement. Looking at him, so healthy and agile, I believed he was leading an active, carefree life. That is very valuable.

To learn the essential meaning of life, we must try not to burden ourselves with unnecessary worries. Worry contaminates our nature. If we face the world with our pure nature, accept the effects from our previous lives, do what we ought to do and constantly reflect on our own actions, then we are using our innate ability to the fullest extent and making the best use of our lives.

The Content Father
and the Thief

You have to be content before you can be tranquil. Only by having few desires and being content can you accommodate everything.

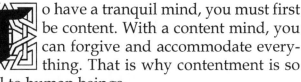o have a tranquil mind, you must first be content. With a content mind, you can forgive and accommodate everything. That is why contentment is so vital to human beings.

In a small village in Japan, there lived a poor, young husband and wife and their three young children. The couple worked very hard to provide for the family. Rain or shine, the husband would go to work before dawn and return home in the evening. But though he worked for long hours, his income could only provide the family a hand-to-mouth existence. The young wife stayed home to take care of her three children and did odd jobs to supplement her husband's income.

Then winter came. The children wore thin clothes and their cheeks turned from red to purple with frostbite. The comforters on their beds were also thin and tattered. The mother's heart ached to see her children in this state.

She hastily collected some wood, with which she made a fire to warm up the house. Her children's faces glowed, reflecting the flickering fire, and she felt somewhat consoled. Though her family was terribly poor, her husband and children gave her a great deal of spiritual support. They were the greatest fortune in her life. With such thoughts in her mind, a satisfied smile appeared on her face.

At that time, she had taken on a job of making a cotton-padded coat for a customer. The material was a fine piece of cloth, which she layered with cotton. She thought: "Once the coat is completed, it will be worn by some fortunate child." As she sewed, she prayed for the child who was going to wear the coat.

But when she saw her own children, she was saddened because she felt powerless to improve their lives. She shook her head and sighed, "When will my children get to wear clothes like this?" She raised her head to check the calendar and thought: "The New Year is coming. I have to hurry up so that this child can wear the new coat on New Year's Eve."

She worked hard and finally finished the coat late in the night. Looking at her husband and children sound asleep, she felt satisfied. She thought, "I will get paid when I hand in the coat tomorrow. The New Year is coming. With the pay, I can buy something nice for the children for New Year." With such thoughts, she fell asleep peacefully.

At midnight, a thief sneaked into their house. The husband heard noises and turned around to take a look. He just caught sight of the thief about to make his escape with the new coat in his hand. The husband got up at once and whispered, "Wait a moment, please." Hearing the voice behind him, the thief turned back, frightened and uneasy.

"Please come inside!" the husband said. But the thief knelt down at the doorway and kowtowed. "Please forgive me. I had no other choice because my father has no winter clothes. If I don't find something for him to wear, he will freeze to death."

"It is cold outside," the husband said gently. "Come and talk inside." Only then did the thief walk into the house, trembling from both cold and fear.

The husband saw that the thief was young. "I really sympathize with you," he said to him. "However, the coat you just took belongs to someone else. Although I don't have anything valuable and my clothes are old, as long as they are helpful to your father, you may take them if you want. There are also a few grains of rice that you can have. In these harsh times, everyone is poor! But my children and I are strong enough to make it through the winter, while your father is old and indeed needs some warm clothing. Go ahead and take what you need."

The thief kowtowed again and again. "How kind you are! You also live in such abject poverty, but you give me things rather than blame me. Thank you so much!" He took the rice and a piece of clothing that his father could wear. When he was leaving, the husband advised him, "Young man, don't steal again! We ought to live with dignity despite our poverty and earn a living through our own efforts. Don't do this again." The thief promised him and left, embarrassed yet grateful.

Smiling, the husband placed the cotton coat next to his wife's pillow. He felt so happy that his wife's efforts would pay off in the end and she could be compensated for her work tomorrow. He felt even more satisfied when he gazed at his good wife and adorable children. What more could he ask for and what did his hardships mean when he had such a lovely family?

Although the family was poor, they were satisfied with what they had. Life should be about contentment. You can be poor but happy, and you can do without material goods but not without integrity. A life like this is truly beautiful!

Father and Son

You should be honest at all times, because honesty is the best bridge between people.

onesty is the best bridge between people. Without mutual honesty, even close relationships such as those between father and son or husband and wife will be broken.

There was once a father and son who loved and cared for each other very much. But they never expressed their feelings. Sometimes the son would do something against his father's will even though he knew that his father loved him and he in turn loved his father. But he wanted to be independent and he didn't want to be restricted, so he often disobeyed his father.

One day, the father thought, "What am I going to do with such a willful son? After I die, he probably won't make my funeral arrangements the way I want. I have to think of some way to solve this problem..." The father wanted to be buried in the mountains, where he could see the world from above. However, he thought, "If I ask him to bury me in the mountains, he will surely bury me beside the river."

So he came up with an idea that he thought was quite brilliant. He said to his son, "I don't ask much of you, only that you honor my wish to be buried by the river." The son bore his father's request in mind, even though he still worried his father with his rebellious behavior.

Some years later, the father passed away. The son thought, "Why did I always provoke my father when he was still alive? I was really a bad son! If I had known that he would pass away so early, I would have made him happy every day." The son regretted that he had never expressed his love for his father.

He was willing to honor his father's wish of being buried by the river. But he worried that his father's coffin might be washed out if heavy rain should cause the river to rise. However, since it was his father's last wish, he had no other choice but to bury him at the riverbank.

After the funeral was over, the son still worried every day. Whenever the sky became cloudy, he was anxious that it would rain. He could often be seen pacing back and forth on the riverbank. He blamed himself bitterly for not having treated his father better and he was even too distressed to eat anything. Before long, he died by his father's grave.

After the young man passed away, people often saw a big bird hovering over the father's grave. The rumor went around the village that the big bird was actually the young man, who felt so regretful and worried that he lingered by the grave every single day, calling out, "Father, father."

Like his dishonest son, the father also said things that he didn't mean and so he was buried by the river. This story is a reminder that everyone should honestly express what he or she thinks. We should nurture this honesty in order to get along well with others.

The Winter Sun

Love can drive away cold indifference. Timely assistance is like the warmth of the winter sun.

old weather always gives one a sense of bleakness. Every time the weather turns cold, I think to myself, "The rich have cotton or leather clothes to keep themselves warm, but some poor families live in houses that can barely shelter them from the wind and rain and don't have any warm clothes or comforters. It is really hard for them to get through the winter."

Tzu Chi relief work in mainland China is always carried out at the beginning of winter. It snows and is freezing cold in winter there. Then there are natural disasters that make people's lives even harder in poverty-stricken areas.

However, heart-warming events also take place amidst the miserable circumstances. A figure often comes to my mind. It is of an old man who looked to be in his seventies. On a day when the snow was falling heavily, this old man only had on a coat with all the buttons missing and a pair of shoes that were split open in front.

He waited in the crowd to receive relief supplies, cringing from the cold. Our commissioners caught sight of him and went to tend to him.

He said, "I haven't eaten anything in days because we have nothing at home. I set out last night and walked here to get supplies."

The commissioners felt very sorry for the old man and immediately wrapped a heavy winter coat around him. Seeing that his hands were still trembling, they also found some bread for him to eat.

On receiving the bread, the toothless old man immediately put it in his mouth. He was still shivering as he ate it. Tzu Cheng Faith Corps members immediately passed him a cup of hot tea. His hand kept shaking and he was unable to drink the tea, so one of the commissioners held the cup to his mouth for him. The old man drank the hot tea and held the bread in one hand. Tears streamed down his cheek, and the commissioners wiped his face with a warm towel. It is a scene that has left a deep impression on me.

I also read a touching story once. There was a small village in which most of the inhabitants were very poor. However, even though they all lived in the same poverty, they had very different values.

It was dusk on a very cold day. Every household kept the doors and windows shut tight to keep out the strong winds and whirling snow. An old man wearing shabby clothes and a pair of straw sandals tottered in the snow, trying to get a cup of hot tea from anyone who would give him one. However, he was rejected at every household and was about to collapse from cold and fatigue. Somehow, he mustered up his last strength and staggered on.

Finally, the old man came to a cottage, the door of which was also fastened tight. Exhausted and unable to go on any longer, he had no other choice but to summon his courage and knock on the door.

Someone inside answered, "Who is it?" The door was opened by an old woman. Seeing the pale, trembling old man, the old woman immediately helped him in, saying, "Why did you come outdoors in such freezing weather? Come in!"

 - She sat the old man down and said, "I have nothing here, not even a fire, but at least it's warmer here than outside. Don't worry! You can rest here."

"I'm very hungry because I've had nothing to eat for days on end," the old man said to her. "Could you spare me something to eat?"

The old woman said, "I know you're hungry, but I haven't had anything since last night, either. Anyway, I can go out to find some food for you. Just rest here."

The old woman braved the snowstorm and knocked on her neighbors' doors one by one. However, it was so cold that some neighbors refused even to open the doors, while others answered the door but had no food to give her. The old woman felt helpless and thought, "If I go back empty-handed, the old man will die of starvation! What should I do?"

She walked on and saw a vegetable garden. An idea suddenly occurred to her. "I can grub up some vegetables for the old man. Although I can only boil them in plain water, they can more or less help him regain energy. But the garden belongs to someone else. What should I do?" She thought again, "If I don't get any vegetables, the old man will surely die!"

She struggled between the two choices, but in the end decided that saving a life was more important. She dug up a big turnip from the garden and murmured happily, "God bless the old man! He can finally enjoy a delicious bowl of turnip soup." Satisfied, she hurried home at once.

The next morning, the owner of the garden found a hole in the ground and knew that one of his turnips had been stolen. "Even though he only stole a turnip, he's still a thief," he cried. "We mustn't allow any thieves in our village." People from the neighboring gardens all gathered around him. "There must be a thief in the neighborhood," he said. "We have to track him down at once. Look! The footprints are still visible!"

"That's right," someone chimed in. "If the thief stole from this garden, he might steal from my garden the next time. We can't allow any thieves here." So the group followed the footprints in search of the culprit.

As they began searching, snow suddenly started to fall swiftly and heavily, and it soon completely covered the footprints. The villagers couldn't find the footprints no matter how hard they looked.

This story gives one contrasting feelings: the bitter coldness of winter and the warmth of humanity.

Love can drive away cold indifference. If everyone can cultivate compassionate love and help others, there may be much less sadness and sorrow in the world.

Take a Step Back

As long as you are able to play your own role well, there is no need to quarrel with others. Too many arguments will erode the affection between people.

t dawn, I listen quietly to the singing of birds and frogs, so pleasant and rhythmic, as though they were holding a wonderful musical concert. How beautiful the sight is of the rising sun casting its light upon the green grass! What a blessed world it would be if all people lived in such serene surroundings and were in harmony with each other!

Unfortunately, many people do not know how to enjoy a beautiful day in such pleasant surroundings. They are always dissatisfied and argue with others, which leads to many worries. I often say, "If you want to get along well with people, you should refrain from arguing or fighting with them. If you want things to continue smoothly, don't contend over every matter. If you want peace and harmony in the world, don't become involved in any conflict."

Some may say, "Reason is on my side." But in fact, too much reasoning with others can wear out the affection between you and them.

Do not mind others too much as long as you know where you stand and perform your role well. Don't be too concerned about personal gains or losses. When you stop asking for more, you will find you are getting more. This is why we say, "Take a step back and discover a world as boundless as the sea and sky."

Someone once told me a true story about a couple who loved each other and their children dearly. They did not want their children to undergo the pressure of the joint entrance examinations for college in Taiwan, so they decided to let their children study abroad. In order to take care of the kids, the wife immigrated to Canada with them. At first, the husband visited them often. When he was in Taiwan, he would phone his wife every day and say, "You are enduring a lot for the children. Thank you." The wife also consoled her husband by saying, "You are also working hard for all of us in Taiwan." In brief, they were thoughtful and close to each other despite the distance between them.

But the husband gradually started to phone his wife less and less. Then for a period of time, she didn't hear from her husband at all. This silence aroused her suspicion, so she called him in Taiwan one day. It was early morning in Taiwan, and to her surprise the person who answered the phone was her husband's secretary! The wife asked her, "Why are you in my house so early in the morning?"

The secretary replied with no signs of embarrassment in her voice, "Why not? I'm living with your husband."

The wife was so shocked she almost fainted. She said angrily, "How could you do something like this?"

"Your husband has nobody to take care of him. Besides, we love and understand each other. Why shouldn't we live together?"

The wife gnashed her teeth in fury and slammed down the phone. She absolutely could not tolerate this scandalous behavior and later called her husband at his office to confront him. But her husband acted as though it was no big deal. Even more irritated, the wife asked, "Are you never coming to visit us in Canada again? Are you going to leave us for good?" He answered, "Yes!" And what an effortless "Yes" it was.

The wife hung up the phone again. From then on, she lived in extreme misery and cried every day. She kept wondering how things had turned out so bad when they had been so happy together? Her daughter found out about the affair and suggested, "Mom, what's the use of you being angry here? Why don't you go back to Taiwan and collect evidence of their adultery?" She accepted the suggestion and flew back to Taiwan. After gathering sufficient proof, she sued the secretary for adultery.

But the cunning secretary unabashedly declared that she was six months pregnant with the husband's child and demanded a fair settlement. Thus the dispute dragged on.

Her husband took sides with the secretary, and the lonely, helpless wife could only go back to Canada. Despondent, she thought, "What is love? What is the meaning of life?" The more she dwelled on her woes, the more depressed she became, to the point of feeling physically ill.

Later on, she remembered that her children still needed her and she could not afford to collapse. At that time, a friend said to her, "Let's go out and do something that will contribute to society and make our lives more happy and meaningful." She thought, "Indeed, we have to do something meaningful with our lives, or we will have come into this world for nothing." As a result, she became a volunteer for the Tzu Chi branch office in Vancouver and devoted herself to social work.

From the cases she was involved in, she witnessed much of the suffering in the world. Some of the lonely old people she helped used to live wonderful lives in the past but were forlorn in their old age. Her perspective was broadened through her work and she realized that life had been good to her. At least she still had three considerate children. There was nothing more to complain about.

She became more at peace with her situation and lived each day happily. Almost a year went by, during which time she occasionally wrote or sent photos of her and the three children to her husband.

One day, her husband suddenly went to see them in Canada. He asked her, "Do you think you could tie a yellow ribbon on the tree to welcome me back?" The wife answered, "Yes, welcome back!" The husband felt so guilty towards his wife that he kept apologizing to her. Then, during Chinese New Year, the husband invited his wife and children to come back to spend their vacation with him in Taiwan.

It turned out that the secretary had left him and taken the child with her. What had happened? During that year, the husband kept reflecting on his actions and felt that he had done wrong, while the secretary quarreled with him incessantly, demanding that he divorce his wife and marry her. She even hid the letters his wife wrote him. He felt that she had become impossible to live with. They quarreled constantly and finally broke up. In the end, the wife agreed to get back together with her husband and start anew.

It is because of the wife's generosity and broadmindedness that this story had a happy ending. Don't reason with others too much, or the affection and bond between you may deteriorate. In daily life, we should learn to be accommodating. Even when reason is on your side, you should still try to be soft-spoken and forgiving. One who can lead a safe, peaceful life is the most fortunate.

The Bondage of Love

You will be plagued with endless worries if you cling to small, personal love. On the contrary, great love for all people can make you peaceful and happy.

young lady accompanied by her mother and a Tzu Chi commissioner came to visit me one day. She seemed weighed down by heavy thoughts. Even though many people had tried to counsel and comfort her, she still looked extremely depressed. "I'm really worried about her," her mother told me. "She drinks every day and physically abuses herself after getting drunk. I really don't know what to do."

I asked the young woman, "Why are you so full of hate?"

She replied, "How can I not hate? My husband deserted me. When we first fell in love, he was so considerate and gentle. But not long after we got married and I was pregnant, he had an affair and left me. How can I not be angry? How can I not hate?"

She seemed to be consumed by her hatred and even said, "He not only deserted our child and me, but also left behind some debts. I wish I could kill him right now." One commissioner present had gone through a similar situation and had been in the same state of mind, so she counseled this young woman with her own experience.

At that moment, a young man came to see me. He was a graduate student at a renowned institute with a promising future ahead of him.

I asked him, "Is something troubling you?"

"I'm troubled by my love for my girlfriend," he said. "I can't forget her. I can't find any reason to go on living."

A commissioner said to me, "He has tried several times to commit suicide. Now, he can't keep his mind on his studies."

I said to him, "Does your love for your girlfriend really carry so much weight in your heart?"

"Yes, we've been together for many years."

"Many years? Then tell me how much that love weighs. Can you weigh it? Can you show me where it is?"

Something seemed suddenly to strike him. "That's it! It has no weight."

"Since it has no weight, why should you die for her? Can you really not live without the girl? Will the world fall apart without her? The person who truly deserves your love is someone who loves you faithfully. If she really loved you, she wouldn't marry another man. Since she doesn't love you, why should you suffer because of her and torture yourself?"

"I see," he said to me. "You want me to concentrate on my studies, right?"

"Exactly! If you live with the correct attitude toward life, then a bright future is yours to create. You can make good use of your knowledge and work for the welfare of all. You had the courage to take your own life. Why not use that courage instead to make a great commitment to work for society? Live on for both yourself and others!"

"Now I understand," the young man said. "I should find myself again and concentrate on my studies."

People are often disconcerted by unrequited love or petty concerns to the point of harming themselves or others. To me, this is such a waste of life. The point is, only when you open your mind and carry out your duties in earnest can you find the true value of your life. If you indulge in small, personal love, your life will be an unhappy one.

A Bowl of Noodles

A prison sentence has a time limit, but psychological suffering is a lifelong infliction.

There was once a couple who often fought over little trifles. Neither was ever willing to give in first, so no one won in the end. One day, the husband went out drinking and returned home long after his wife had gone to sleep. But feeling hungry, he woke up his wife and asked her to make a bowl of noodles for him. So the wife got up to fix him some noodles. However, when the noodles were ready, the husband had fallen dead asleep and could not be awakened. She left the noodles on the table and went back to bed.

When the husband woke up and discovered that the noodles had become cold, he flew into a fury and began yelling at his wife. His wife yelled right back at him. In the end, husband and wife quarreled over a bowl of noodles in the middle of the night.

During the quarrel, the wife yelled out of spite, "If you are so angry, come and kill me." She threw a knife over to her husband saying, "See if you dare to kill me." Then she walked into the bathroom.

The husband, not yet sobered up, picked up the knife in a fit of anger and followed his wife into the bathroom. He turned off the light and stabbed her. Not knowing where he had wounded her, he only heard a cry of bitter pain. When he turned on the light, he found that she had fallen to the floor and was bleeding profusely.

Still under the influence of alcohol, he kept telling his wife, "Get up! Get up!" But when his wife didn't answer, he realized how bad the situation was and hastily called an ambulance. But his wife died before she arrived at the hospital.

The husband completely regretted what he had done. A life had been lost over a bowl of noodles and the husband was sentenced to prison. The prison term eventually came to an end, but he blamed himself for the rest of his life. It is more painful to be punished mentally than physically. And all this was caused by the couple's hot tempers and hurtful words. If the wife had understood that her husband was drunk and ignored his verbal attacks, she would not have given him the knife and the tragedy would not have ensued.

Nowadays, people often cause tragedies that they regret for the rest of their lives because they cannot tolerate and accommodate others. Therefore, if we wish to avoid doing things that we will feel sorry about, we should learn to treat others with soft words and a moderate attitude. It all depends on carefully cultivating our speech and behavior.

Section 6
The Love of All Living Beings

The Love of
All Living Beings

*Whether a group of people can coexist in harmony
depends on whether the individuals in the group can
respect and accommodate each other.*

n a zoological research institute in
Europe, there was a researcher who
concentrated his studies on chickens.
He examined the behavior and living
patterns of all kinds of chickens. One day, he
found some eggs laid by a pheasant in the woods
and took some of them back to the institute.

At that time, a hen at the institute had just laid
eggs too. The researcher replaced those with the
pheasant eggs. When the hen saw the pheasant
eggs, she hesitated for a moment but then sat on
them as tenderly as though they were her own.

In time, the eggs hatched and out came the
baby pheasants. The mother hen led them to the
woods, where she dug into the dirt with her
claws and searched for worms. When she found
worms, she would call for the baby pheasants
to come over and eat.

Since the research institute had always given
artificial feed to the hen's chicks, the researcher
was very surprised when he observed that the

hen knew the baby pheasants ate only natural food and took care of them accordingly.

The researcher brought in several duck eggs for the mother hen to hatch. The hen, like before, sat on the eggs patiently until they hatched. She then led the baby ducks to a lake for them to swim in.

These two examples taught the researcher that feathered creatures are not senseless, unfeeling animals as he had previously imagined. They are actually loving and wise.

Different people have different personalities, habits and concepts. These differences are the major reasons that lead to conflicts and misunderstandings.

Whether a group of people can get along depends on whether the individuals who constitute that group can respect and accommodate each other. The group will be peaceful and harmonious only when its members can be broad-minded, help each other, and resolve disputes with wisdom, instead of complaining and fighting.

If a mother hen could treat those which were not of its kind with love and wisdom, then as long as we make an effort we should also be able to treat each other with contentment, gratitude, understanding and an accommodating mind.

The Old Man in Search of Treasure

It is better to polish the mirror of your heart than to search outside of yourself for the buddha-nature. If there is love in your heart, then you are a buddha.

n Japan, a high school student who lived in the city went to his uncle's home in the countryside for summer vacation. His uncle's house was located in a rustic village surrounded by beautiful mountains and rivers.

On the first day the student arrived, he and his cousin went out early in the morning to see the sun rise over the sea. As the golden sun rose slowly from the horizon and shone brightly on everything in the area, they gazed with fascination at the gleaming circles of ripples widening on the surface of the sea. Fully mesmerized by the wonder and magnificence of nature, the two young men got up early the next couple of days and went out before daybreak to pay tribute to the beautiful sea. Gradually, the high school student became familiar with the roads and learned how to get to the beach on his own.

One morning he went to the sea alone. Admiring the fascinating view of the sun rising from the sea, he lay down on a boulder and let the breeze gently brush his face.

Just as he was enjoying all this, an old man startled him by suddenly emerging from behind. "Sorry, sorry, I came to look for something—I didn't mean to scare you," the old man apologized absentmindedly.

Seeing that the intruder was completely occupied with his search, the student went on enjoying the picturesque scenery and he even began to whistle. The sound of his whistling mingled with that of the lapping waves engrossed him. Suddenly, he heard someone chanting "Amitabha." He rose to see what was going on and found that the sound came from the old man, who was chanting away while still busily engaged in his search.

When the old man drew near, the boy could no longer suppress his curiosity. "What are you looking for, old man?" he asked.

"I've been looking for this thing for a long time," he answered. "Almost my entire life has been spent on this quest."

"What on earth are you looking for?"

"I'm trying to find something left behind by a saint."

"Which saint? And what did he leave behind?" The boy grew even more interested.

"It was left behind by Master Sinnrann, founder of the Japanese Pure Land sect," the old man said. He pointed to the base of a cliff some distance away. "A long time ago, the Master came to a cave there to enjoy the seascape. Absorbed, he failed to notice that the tide was rising. The brimming tide kept him in that cave for seven days, during which time he picked many stones and engraved 'Amitabha' on them. I believe some of those stones must still be lying around. My longtime wish has been to find them."

After hearing what he said, the boy gazed at the preoccupied old man. But the old man only said to him, "Young man, you are a good boy." Then he went on with his search, combing every inch of the earth. The student stared after the receding figure of the old man and fell into pensive meditation.

The boy's cousin had noticed that he had not yet returned and came looking for him on the beach. The boy told his cousin about his encounter with the old man and asked him, "Is it really possible to find stones with engravings by Master Sinnrann?"

"You silly boy! Master Sinnrann lived hundreds of years ago. For something that happened in such an ancient time, who can be sure how much truth there is to it?"

Whether it was true or not, the old man had spent a good part of his life looking for stones with "Amitabha" carved on them. Wouldn't it have been better to seize the day and look into his own heart for the "Amitabha" that was within him? Wouldn't that have made better use of his time? We should face reality and live in the present with a down-to-earth attitude. Do not dwell on past events or dream vainly about the future. What is important is to hold on to this very moment.

The Woman with Distorted Religious Beliefs

If you can cultivate the correct belief and accommodate everything with a broad mind, you will be blessed with a full and beautiful life.

I often say to people, "As long as you have a tranquil mind and a righteous attitude, you will be impervious to every evil in the world." Having correct beliefs and ways of thinking will keep evil forces at bay. If we want to be wise and be able to tell right from wrong, we should first establish correct beliefs. People in modern-day society often feel empty inside. Understandably, they seek a spiritual shelter.

There was a well-educated couple who enjoyed a good reputation in cultural circles. Because the husband had to take care of his business abroad, he only came home once in a while.

In her husband's absence, the wife often found life monotonous. So when a friend introduced her to a religious group, she enthusiastically took part in its activities. She was so devoted to the religion that her thought, life, speech and behavior were all greatly influenced by it and she became very prejudiced against other religions. She said statues of the buddhas were embodiments of devils and called those who worshipped them demon worshippers. When she found out that someone had a different religious belief from her, she would shun that person and say, "You are worshipping devils." She became impossible to get along with.

What possessed her? Had she lost her mind? But she certainly had not lost her artistic talent. When her husband returned home from abroad and began to transfer his business back to Taiwan, he found that his home was no longer like a home. His wife's behavior and language had completely changed. He could no longer find anything in common with her.

The husband felt helpless. During these years, he had paid too high a price for success. Because he was ambitious and eager to advance his business, he had spent far too much time abroad. But all his efforts had gone down the drain. After so many years of hard work, he now had nothing. More depressing was that when he gave up his overseas businesses to return home, he found that his home was no longer what it had been.

The above example is not unusual in today's society. When even intellectuals make a mistake in choosing a religion, it is very hard to backtrack.

When we choose to believe in a certain religion, what is important is to learn from it how to conduct ourselves in life and improve our relationships with other people. No matter how hostile the environment is or how unfriendly people are, we should accept everything with a broad mind. Only in this way can we stand more firm and assured in our belief.

Be very careful what you choose to believe — this is what you should bear in mind when you practice Buddhism or other religions. Focus on how to interact with people and carry out your duties. Do not pursue supernatural or other-worldly concerns, for it will be dangerous if you indulge yourself in such impractical affairs. Only when we nurture great love and only when people treat each other with love can we all live in happiness.

The Daydreams
of a Little Girl

"Let bygones be bygones; let the future take its course." Eliminate delusions about the past and future and live fully in the present.

Many people dream about their futures. "How wonderful my life will be in the future," they often think. Some years ago I read a children's story about a little Indian girl whose family was poor and who had to work even though she was only twelve or thirteen years old.

One day she went to a market carrying a basket of fruit on her head. While walking through the market, the little girl looked around her and thought, "How wonderful it is to be rich! Rich women live in beautiful houses and dress lavishly every day. Their lives must be so easy and carefree! When I grow up I hope I can dress up every day. Better still, a prince could choose me to be his wife. Then I would be able to live in a palace. How wonderful!"

She dreamed on happily as if she were already in the palace. She pictured the prince inviting her to dance, and she pretended to refuse by coyly shaking her head. Rapt in her daydream, the girl forgot about the basket on her head. As she shook her head, the ripe fruit all fell to the ground and smashed. She looked at the crushed fruit and thought regretfully, "It was all just a dream."

Everyone has plans and aspirations for the future. It is inevitable that we wonder how our futures will turn out. But too much wondering about the future can disturb our minds. Unreal fantasies can obscure our pure, good nature. As Buddhists, we should try to eliminate illusions and concentrate wholeheartedly on the present.

We should understand that dwelling on the past and the future only unsettles our minds. Concentrate on the present. If you can keep your heart as clear as a polished mirror, you will be able to see this world without distortion.

The Story of a Child

When you lose even the ability to cry, what more is there to argue about in life?

There was once a very young patient at the Tzu Chi General Hospital. Only a little over a year old, he was paralyzed. He had been a lively child. One day his mother was holding his hand and teaching him to walk in front of their house. When she let go of him to let him try walking on his own, the child walked towards the street and was hit by a truck.

When the child was taken to the hospital, he had no external injuries but he was not breathing. He regained consciousness after first aid was given to him, but a couple of days later the doctor found that he had not moved his limbs at all. As children ought to be lively and restless, the doctor suspected something was wrong and decided to examine him again. This time the doctor found that the child's spine was ruptured. The poor child was paralyzed and might never be able to breathe without an artificial respirator.

I went to the hospital to see this chubby, lovely child. When I touched his cheeks and called his name, he knew that someone was looking at him and talking to him, but he could not respond. Only his hand could give a little twitch. He could not turn his head either, so the only way he could respond to me was by rolling his eyeballs. I looked at him and saw tears rolling down his cheeks. It made my heart ache.

"Is he able to utter any sound when he cries?" I asked the doctor.

"I'm afraid not," answered the doctor.

This child was so young. At his age, he should have been asking for food when he was hungry and wanting people to hold him and pamper him. But now he couldn't even breathe on his own or cry out, let alone make people know what he needed. What if he got hungry or wanted someone to hold him? Would anyone know?

"Will he be like this for the rest of his life?" I asked the doctor again.

"It will be very difficult for him to get better, but we are all keeping our fingers crossed." The doctor had no alternative but to hope for a miracle.

The child was growing bigger by the day. Apart from giving medical treatment, the doctors also had to watch his weight. If he got too hefty, breathing would become even more difficult for him. In addition, overweight people are more likely to develop bedsores. So it was necessary to monitor the amount of food the child was fed.

"For a child as young as he is, if his spine had the chance to grow normally again, how long would it take for it to function?" I asked the doctor again.

"The spine grows less than one millimeter a day," said the doctor. "So if there were any chance that his spine could grow, it would take at least three years for it to regain its normal functions. But the chances are very slim."

Will this child be able to recover within three years? Even if he can, these three years will be excruciatingly long for him. But that is life.

Looking at this child, I was deeply struck by the impermanence of life. Who can predict what might happen the next moment that will change one's life forever? So what is there to fight over in life? What right do we have to claim that we own our lives? We had better seize the moment and make the best of what we have. Understand that we have only the right to use our lives. That is the only way that we can come to terms with impermanence.

Grandma Learns to Read

Gross errors often arise from minor acts of carelessness. Don't act heedlessly just because you think the matters you are taking care of are unimportant.

 few years ago, a grandmother brought her seven-year-old grandson, who had just entered elementary school, to see me at the Abode of Still Thoughts. The grandmother told me that although her grandson was still very young, he already knew how to treat people properly and had even given her a lesson on it.

At home, the grandson often asked her, "Grandma, why can't you read?" [Actually, this is not uncommon among the older generation in Taiwan.]

"I've lived to this old age and yet my grandson often laughs at me for not being able to read," Grandma thought. "This is really embarrassing." So she decided to attend classes to learn how to read.

But the old woman's memory was failing, and she had trouble remembering the pronunciation of each character. She often had to ask her grandson how to read them.

Once she again forgot how to read a word, so she called to her grandson playfully, "Come here, little one." But her grandson only glanced at her and refused to go to her.

The grandmother walked over to him and asked, "Why didn't you come to me when I called you?"

"Who were you calling to?" inquired the grandson.

"You, of course. Why didn't you come over?"

"Grandma, my name is not 'little one.' It is condescending to address people like that. Besides, you asked me to teach you, so I am your teacher. If you call me 'little one,' how can you possibly remember what I teach you? From what I have learned at school, one should show respect for one's teacher."

The grandma was surprised to hear such an answer. "My grandson is marvelous—just like a young teacher," thought the grandma. She took her grandson's hand and said, "Thank you, little teacher, you have taught me a lesson."

The boy was only in first grade, but because he kept his teacher's words in mind, what he said made sense and impressed his grandmother.

We should try to be sensible when we deal with others. Take the grandmother and grandson for example—they both acted very reasonably. Now the old woman can read very well because she paid attention to every detail and every word her grandson told her. No wonder she could learn so well.

People often live superficially. They go about their daily activities without paying attention to subtle matters such as their thoughts. Actually, what we say and do originate from what we think. Only when we think correctly will our speech and behavior be appropriate. Therefore, it is necessary to constantly monitor our thoughts. Whatever we are doing—talking, working, even walking or eating—we should be discreet in our behavior. If we are able to do so, we will be cultivating ourselves to be good Buddhists and we will be imbued in the pure stream of Buddhism.

On the contrary, if we neglect our minds and let greed, anger or delusions arise, we will cause ourselves a lot of trouble. Sometimes one careless remark can have a significant effect on ourselves and others. The importance of the attention we should pay to subtle activities of the mind cannot be overemphasized.

"One stray thought leads to untold wrongs." Gross errors often originate from minor acts of carelessness. Don't act heedlessly just because you think the matters you are taking care of are unimportant. Small actions convey important messages. Therefore, "Don't lapse into evil deeds just because they are small; don't avoid doing good deeds just because they are insignificant." You should put your heart into everything you do.

The Magical Clogs

Harbor good intentions and be content, then you will attain wisdom. Allow one greedy thought and you will suffer from unfulfilled desires.

here was once a mother and son who depended upon each other. The son was a good boy who was very respectful towards his mother. When he was about seven, his mother suddenly fell seriously ill. They were poor and could not afford a doctor. The little boy was very anxious but did not know what to do.

His mother would surely die if she didn't receive immediate treatment. At the end of his wits, the boy could only think of borrowing money from his sole relative, his uncle. But when the uncle learned that the boy wanted to borrow money from him, he pulled a long face.

"Children should not borrow money from other people," said the uncle.

"But if I don't, my mother will die," answered the boy. "You are my last hope."

"Are you trying to swindle money from me?" snapped the uncle. "Don't expect me to lend you anything."

The tearful boy kept imploring his uncle to show some sympathy. Finally, the uncle gave in reluctantly. "Alright, I'll lend you the money. But don't you ever come back asking for more."

The boy only got a little money from his uncle, barely enough to pay for a dose of medicine. Even so, the boy thanked his uncle profusely and kept kowtowing to him. Then he hurried over to the doctor to ask for a prescription.

His mother got much better after she took the medicine. But one dose was not enough for her to completely regain her health. The little boy could only force himself to go to his uncle again.

This time the uncle not only refused to see him, but he wouldn't even open the door. No matter how hard the boy begged and cried, his uncle kept his door tightly closed.

The little boy waited until nightfall. Then, thinking of his mother alone at home with no one to care for her, he decided to go back. He walked and cried along the way until he bumped into someone. Looking up, he saw an old man.

"I'm sorry. I was feeling so depressed that I didn't see you coming. I'm really sorry." The boy kept bowing and apologizing to the old man.

"Why are you so sad?" asked the old man, and the boy told him what had happened. "You're such a good boy! Don't worry, I'll help you," said the old man, and he took out a pair of wood clogs from his bag.

"Child, when you need money, put on these clogs and take a few steps. When they clatter over the ground, gold and silver will appear before you."

The little boy took the clogs from the old man, but he noticed something unusual. "There's only one supporting wedge on each sole. Can I walk steadily with these?"

"As long as you concentrate and are sincere," answered the old man.

The boy then accepted the clogs respectfully and hopefully.

"You must keep one thing in mind," cautioned the old man. "Once you have enough money, don't try to get any more. After you use the clogs the first time, every time you put them on, your body will shrink."

"Please don't worry. I know how I should use them."

The boy then took the clogs home. When he tried them on as the old gentleman had instructed him, a lot of gold and silver appeared on the ground. Overjoyed, he immediately took off the clogs and sent for the doctor. Under the doctor's care, his mother soon recovered fully.

Some time afterwards, the boy's uncle thought to himself, "I haven't seen the kid for a long time. I wonder if his mother is still alive." Curious, he went to visit them and found that the mother looked healthy and the family's living conditions seemed to have improved.

"How come you're so well off now?" he asked the little boy. "How did your mother recover?" The honest boy told his uncle everything. After he had heard the story, the uncle told the boy to get out the clogs and let him have a look. When he got hold of them, he said, "I don't believe what you have told me is true. In order to stop you from using these clogs to cheat other people, I shall keep them myself."

The uncle took the clogs with him. Although the boy was reluctant to part with them, the uncle was his elder and there was nothing he could do.

After he got home, the uncle couldn't wait to put the clogs on. When he saw that gold and silver indeed appeared on the ground, he was so happy that he kept walking in the clogs. His body gradually shrank, and before he knew it he had become smaller than the clogs. Finally he was reduced to the size of an invisible grain of sand.

In daily life, we often see people who forget their sense of honor the moment they see a chance to get rich. For the sake of money, they say what they should not say and do what they should not do. Do people really have to degrade themselves in order to satisfy their material desires?

The little boy was able to lead a stable, peaceful life because he was content with his lot and never asked for more than he needed. His uncle, on the other hand, was dishonest and avaricious, so the clogs brought him irreparable damage.

I often say, "When you do what you should do, you are wise; when you do what you should not do, you are foolish." And it is one's thoughts that dictate what one should do or should not do.

The story of the magical clogs is a fable, but the message conveyed in it is worth reflecting on.

Rise and Shine

Worldly pleasures are as ephemeral as bubbles or passing clouds. True happiness is attained when you have a clear conscience and peace of mind.

There was a young man who had lost his father when he was very young and had been brought up single-handedly by his mother, who worked hard to provide a solid education for him. Although life was not easy, mother and son had each other to rely on, so they still lived contentedly and happily.

When the son was still a student, his mother would wake him up every morning, saying, "Rise and shine, it's time to go to school!" Even after he had started to work, his mother kept up the habit. "Rise and shine, it's time to go to work!" It was an important daily routine for her.

One day, the son came home after work and said to his mother, "Mom, you've been working too hard. I'm sorry I haven't been able to provide you with a comfortable life. Look at our house—it's so bare and shabby. I'm thinking of starting my own business. If I succeed, I'll be able to renovate our house and buy new furniture and things. You can have anything you want in it."

After hearing her son's words, the mother asked, "Will the money you make be decent money?"

"Yes, it should be. But the way business works can sometimes be unfair to some people."

"Son, I wake you up every morning, right?"

"Yes. Why do you ask?"

"Every morning I make breakfast for you and call you when it is time to get up. But even when I call you several times, you never answer. I have to run upstairs to wake you up. Sometimes you are so sound asleep I even have to shake you awake. Often when you finally open your eyes, you still look like you could fall right back to sleep. Still, waking you up every day gives me a sense of reassurance. I hope I don't find you wide awake when I go to your bed, because that would mean you aren't sleeping well."

The son understood what his mother was saying. "Mom, I see what you mean. Rest assured that I will never do anything to make you worry. No matter how difficult our lives may be, so long as we have a clear conscience we'll be able to live happily, right?"

"Yes," the mother said with a smile. "You will be a truly good son if you can let me live with a clear conscience. We should not want more than what is enough to support ourselves. What is important is to have a clear conscience and peace of mind, because that is where true happiness lies."

This is the correct view of life—making honest money through hard work instead of shrewd business calculations that may weigh heavily on your mind. Otherwise, all the money in the world will not make you happy and at ease.

Worldly pleasures are like bubbles—when you reach out to touch or capture them, they vanish in a flash. Worldly pleasures are also as changeable as clouds in the summertime, impossible to get hold of. As long as you do your duties every day and shut the door that leads to greed and desire, you will live your life in peace and joy.